MILESTONES
IN
AMERICAN HISTORY
★★★★★★★★★★★★★

THE RAID ON
HARPERS FERRY

MILESTONES
IN
AMERICAN HISTORY

MILESTONES
IN
AMERICAN HISTORY

THE RAID ON HARPERS FERRY

JOHN BROWN'S REBELLION

SAMUEL WILLARD CROMPTON

CHELSEA HOUSE
PUBLISHERS
An imprint of Infobase Publishing

The Raid on Harpers Ferry

Chelsea House
An imprint of Infobase Publishing
132 West 31st Street
New York, NY 10001

Library of Congress Cataloging-in-Publication Data

Crompton, Samuel Willard.
The raid on Harpers Ferry : John Brown's rebellion / Samuel Willard Crompton.
  p. cm.— (Milestones in American history)
Includes bibliographical references and index.
ISBN 978-1-60413-678-4 (hardcover)
1. Harpers Ferry (W. Va.)—History—John Brown's Raid, 1859—Juvenile literature.
2. Brown, John, 1800–1859—Juvenile literature. I. Title.
E451.C93 2010
973.7'116—dc22   2009036994

Text design by Erik Lindstrom
Cover design by Alicia Post
Composition by Keith Trego
Cover printed by Bang Printing, Brainerd, MN
Book printed and bound by Bang Printing, Brainerd, MN
Date printed: February 2011
Printed in the United States of America

10 9 8 7 6 5 4 3 2

CONTENTS

George Washington's Sword

Forty-six-year-old Lewis Washington, a colonel in the Virginia militia, was awakened at 1:30 in the morning by a loud sound from the rear of the house. Clad in his night-clothes, Colonel Washington went to the back, where he met four men who had broken down the door. Three of them carried rifles, and the fourth had a large revolver. One carried a large torch. Colonel Washington later described the event to a special congressional committee: "The person in command turned out to be [Aaron] Stevens. He asked me my name, and then referred to a man of the name of Cook, who had been at my house before, to know whether I was Colonel Washington. On being told that I was, he said, 'You are our prisoner.'"[1]

This was quite astonishing since both the Commonwealth of Virginia and the United States of America were at peace.

COLONEL WASHINGTON.—[Drawn by Porte Crayon.]

Colonel Lewis Washington, great-grandnephew of George Washington, was the first prisoner taken hostage by John Brown's men. Lewis Washington, his male slaves, and the sword of Frederick the Great were taken to the engine house.

Colonel Washington, however, began to put two and two together; he remembered that this man "Cook" had been at his house a few weeks before and that he had shown great curiosity in some relics and mementos in the colonel's possession. As the great-grandnephew of George Washington, the nation's first president, Colonel Washington had enjoyed first choice when it came to selecting souvenirs of his famous relative. He had chosen President Washington's pair of pistols (given to the president by the Marquis de Lafayette) and his ceremonial sword (sent to the president by Frederick the Great, King of Prussia). Cook had asked about the pistols, and Colonel Washington had shown them to him.

As he explained to the congressional investigative committee, Colonel Washington had been frightened at first, but he mustered his courage to tell the men that they were very bold fellows, thanks to the weapons they possessed. He added, though, "I believe with a pop-gun I could take either of you in your shirt tail."[2] This act of bravado did not impress the intruders, and Colonel Washington went on to ask why they had come, for it was quite a mystery to him. Stevens spoke up and said, "We have come here for the purpose of liberating all the slaves of the South, and we are able (or prepared) to do it."[3]

If Colonel Washington had been surprised, and then frightened, his feelings now ran to amusement. How did such a slender band of men, armed with nothing more than the weapons of frontier men, think they would bring down the institution of slavery? There were more than 4 million slaves, spread from Maryland to Texas: Who did these fellows think they were?

Part of the answer came from Stevens, who asked Colonel Washington if he had ever heard of Osawatomie Brown. The colonel replied that he had not, to which Stevens answered that he must not have paid much attention to the Kansas Territory over the past few years. Rather indignantly, Colonel Washington said that he was so weary of hearing about the Territory of Kansas—and the troubles between Free State and pro-slavery men—that every time he saw a newspaper with "Kansas" in the headline, he promptly turned it over and refused to read. "'Well,' said he [Stevens], 'you will see him this morning,' speaking apparently with great glorification."[4]

Colonel Washington had already surrendered the sword and pistols of his illustrious relative. Now he was pushed out into the cold, damp night (there was a light rain), where he saw his carriage and his four-horse wagon pulled up. Some of his slaves (apparently the intruders *did* intend to free them all) were there, ready to drive the horse and carriage into the night.

TO THE FERRY

As they all left, Colonel Washington noticed that one of the black men who had come with the intruders held his great-grand-uncle's ceremonial sword. This seemed odd, but then again the entire night was one of strange doings. An hour later, the wagon and carriage approached the federal arsenal at Harpers Ferry, a place where Colonel Washington had been dozens, if not hundreds, of times. Down deep, he still cherished the hope that this was a strange and cruel joke, but when he heard one of the intruders call out "All's well," and receive the answering call of the night watchman, the colonel knew these men were serious. Somehow, by some mix of strategy and risk-taking, they had seized the federal arsenal, which President Washington had established back in the 1790s.

As the carriage pulled into the armory, Colonel Washington was led from it into the courtyard. There he met a rather strange-looking fellow, to whom the intruders showed signs of great deference. The man's first words were, "You will find a fire in here, sir; it is rather cool this morning."[5]

MAN OF MANY NAMES

Entering the arsenal's engine house, Colonel Washington had a chance to examine this man. He was of average height, but his extreme fitness made him seem taller than he was. He also was not young, for the work of a lifetime had knitted deep lines in his forehead. There was something quite different about the man, almost as if he belonged to an earlier, more romantic time.

"I presume you are Mr. Washington," the man said. "I shall be very attentive to you, sir, for I may get the worst of it in my first encounter, and if so, your life is worth as much as mine."[6]

John Brown was clean-shaven until his mid-fifties, the time when he wanted to appear as a Moses-like figure. This photograph was taken a year before the raid on Harpers Ferry, which historians cite as one of the major events that led to the Civil War.

This, of course, was what Colonel Washington wanted to know. What was the first encounter? Why had he been abducted in the night? But something in the stranger's manner made him pause and wait.

"My particular reason for taking you first was that, as the aide to the governor of Virginia, I knew you would endeavor to perform your duty, and perhaps you would have been a troublesome customer to me; and, apart from that, I wanted you particularly for the moral effect it would give our cause, having one of your name as a prisoner."[7]

Light began to dawn. Throughout his life, Colonel Washington had received a great deal of attention and respect because of his connection to George Washington. On this occasion, however, the attention seemed to have a negative connotation. The man who held him captive did not give any lengthy explanation about what the cause entailed, just something to the effect of "this thing must be put a stop to."[8]

He meant slavery.

Though Colonel Washington did not know it yet, he was in the presence of a man who had ignited controversy in the Kansas Territory, in New England, in Ohio, and elsewhere. He was the captive of a rather ruthless and hard man, one who knew a great deal about duty and endeavoring to perform it. Over the next 36 hours, Colonel Washington would hear this man called a number of things, for he had many names.

Brown of Osawatomie

Captain John Brown of Kansas

Old Brown

It is difficult to say which name Brown preferred, for each one carried a piece of his truth. He was indeed Brown of Osawatomie, the feared Free State man from Kansas, and he was also Captain John Brown, who had formed his own militia in imitation of the Founding Fathers. He was also Old Brown, a name that spoke to his age and his position as leader of the Brown clan.

HISTORICAL IRONY

It was ironic that John Brown and his 21 accomplices had abducted Colonel Washington. Brown and most of his men revered the cause of 1776 and held the memory of the American Revolution dear to their hearts. Still, they felt it had not gone far enough and that presidents Washington, Jefferson, and Madison had left a major piece undone: They had allowed slavery to continue. Now, in 1859, 83 years after the Declaration of Independence, Brown and his men would do their best to finish the work of the Founding Fathers.

Brown strapped on George Washington's sword. He would use the great man's legacy to further the building of his own, even while he held that man's relative as a prisoner.

The Ferry

Harpers Ferry is one of the most intriguing and spell-binding of locations. It features a sense of mystery and danger, as well as a visual thrill, as mountains and rivers come together in a scene of natural beauty.

THE FOUNDING OF HARPERS FERRY

Located at the confluence of the Potomac and Shenandoah rivers, Harpers Ferry was doubtless a passing ground for numerous Native American groups until the first white settlers arrived in the 1740s. One, an English immigrant named Robert Harper, created the first rude bridge across the Potomac and built a house or two on the land that is now named for him. Back then, the area was part of the colony of Virginia; today, Harpers Ferry is in the state of West Virginia.

Formerly called Shenandoah Falls at Mr. Harper's Ferry, Harpers Ferry, Virginia (now West Virginia) began as the starting point for settlers moving into the Shenandoah Valley and further west. In 1799, Harpers Ferry was named one of two facilities for national arsenals—the other being Springfield, Massachusetts. They produced most of the small arms for the U.S. Army.

The Potomac comes from the northwest, and the Shenandoah makes an arc from the southwest; when they join, the Potomac becomes much larger, sweeping watercraft of all types along (in springtime, trees and shrubs are often carried off by the freshet, or spring thaw). This combination of mountain, water, and forest was what called Harpers Ferry to the attention of George Washington, Thomas Jefferson, and others.

The young George Washington passed by Harpers Ferry several times, and later in life, he considered the spot and its potential importance to the nation. Elected the first president of the United States in 1789, Washington confronted the painful fact that the country had a small military and virtually no armament.

In 1792, and again in 1794, President Washington proposed three federal arsenals: one at Springfield, Massachusetts, one at Harpers Ferry, and a third at Rocky Mount, South Carolina. In each case, President Washington looked for a location far

A STUPENDOUS SCENE

The passage of the Potomac through the Blue Ridge is perhaps one of the most stupendous scenes in nature. You stand on a very high point of land. On your right comes up the Shenandoah, having ranged along the foot of the mountain an [sic] hundred miles to seek a vent. On your left approaches the Potomac, in quest of a passage also. In the moments of their junction they rush together against the mountain, rend it asunder, and pass off to the sea. The first glance of this scene hurries our senses into the opinion that this earth has been created in time, that the mountains were formed first, that the rivers began to flow afterwards, that in this place particularly they have been damned up by the Blue Ridge of mountains, and have formed an ocean which filled the whole valley; that continuing to rise they have at length broken over at this spot, and have torn the mountain down from its summit to its base.*

Thomas Jefferson was a poet (at heart), a literary craftsman, a keen observer of nature, and the author of the Declaration of enough inland to be safe from the warships of Britain, France, or any other enemy, but close enough to a fine source of water power. Springfield, on the Connecticut River, came first; Rocky Mount was discarded; and Harpers Ferry came second and last. The first arms mechanics moved there in 1799, and the first muskets were turned out in 1801. From that time on, U.S. soldiers—whether they served in the War of 1812, the Mexican War, or the numerous conflicts with Native Americans—generally carried muskets and rifles that were stamped on the butt with either "Springfield" or "Harpers Ferry."

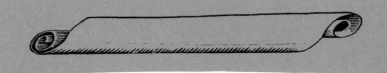

Independence. He wrote this description of Harpers Ferry for his *Notes on the State of Virginia*, published in 1782.

Jefferson was largely correct about the formation of the land and water in this region, one that led to Harpers Ferry being considered distinct—both locally and far and wide. The cooling effects of the two rivers coming together made it a natural spot for vacationers, but in the end it was the military that claimed this special spot.

When he was the third president of the United States (1801–1809), Jefferson sent the explorers Meriwether Lewis and William Clark west. They reached the Pacific Ocean and commented on the land and waters in between. Jefferson was thrilled to read their reports, for though he loved the West like few other people, he never went farther than the summit of the Blue Ridge Mountains.

*Thomas Jefferson, *Notes on the State of Virginia*. New York: The Norton Library, 1954, p. 19.

GROWTH AND DEVELOPMENT

About 2,000 rifles and muskets were turned out that first year, and the number grew steadily over the next two decades. Harpers Ferry, which now included almost all the land sitting between the confluence of the two rivers, saw its population rise to about 1,000 people, some of whom remained for many years, while others were temporary or seasonal workers. Perhaps because of its military mission, the location did not attract artists or poets; unlike the Hudson River, which had an entire artistic group grow up around it, the upper reaches of the Potomac and Shenandoah remained almost secluded.

The armory's growth has been recorded by historians Daniel D. Hartzel and James B. Whisker:

> In 1830 Harpers Ferry produced 10,130 muskets and received $165,567 from the Treasury; and Springfield produced 16,500 muskets, receiving $187,524 from the Treasury. Hall's rifle works [at Harpers Ferry] received a total appropriation of $86,401, with $32,377 of that going to rifle manufacture."[1]

The success of Springfield and Harpers Ferry can be seen in the 1830s, as the leaders of the U.S. military estimated that they had 45,000 serviceable muskets on hand, enough to arm a sizable militia (the regular U.S. Army itself was still quite small). What no one back then expected was that the weapons the two arsenals produced might some day be used by the partisans of a region (North or South) in a civil war.

THE PEOPLE OF THE TOWN

One of our best looks at Harpers Ferry comes from the U.S. Census of 1850, conducted nine years before John Brown's famous raid. Here is a breakdown of the town's population:

White People		Free Black People		Slaves		Total
Male	Female	Male	Female	Male	Female	
806	745	50	37	37	72	1,747[2]

As this indicates, Harpers Ferry was not, by any means, a hotbed of African-American slavery. Let us compare its population figures with those of Richmond, the capital of Virginia, in 1850:

White People		Free Black People		Slaves		Total
Male	Female	Male	Female	Male	Female	
7,783	7,491	1,075	1,294	5,307	4,620	27,570[3]

The figures show that slaves accounted for only 6.2 percent of the total population of Harpers Ferry. In Richmond, slaves made up 36 percent of the population. Clearly, Harpers Ferry was not typical of Virginia. It was, in fact, typical of several mountainous regions that straddled the border between the "free" Northern states and the "slave" Southern states. As a whole, Virginia experienced population and wealth loss during the 1850s, due to a decline in the price of tobacco, but Harpers Ferry and other northern parts of the state felt the impact more than the rest of Virginia.

THE ARMORY ON THE VERGE

John Brown's raid came in October 1859, three months after a dangerous tornado struck Harpers Ferry (the special meeting of mountains and rivers sometimes made the area vulnerable to major displays of weather). Just nine months earlier, Harpers Ferry had received a new superintendent, Alfred M. Barbour. His reports show that about 400 men were employed at the armory, more than enough, it would seem, to repel a raid by John Brown or anyone else. The workers were mainly employed in turning out the Model 1855 U.S. Pistol Carbine.

They did not know, could not have known, that the man who would come, hoping to displace them and to free the slaves, tended to prefer Sharps rifles, made in Northern factories.

YOUNG JOHN BROWN

John Brown was born in Torrington, Connecticut, on May 9, 1800, the son of Owen Brown and Ruth Mills. On his father's side, he was descended from some of the Pilgrims who crossed the ocean to settle in Plymouth, Massachusetts; on his mother's side, he was descended from Dutch and English immigrants.

Much of what we know about Brown's early years is thanks to a 10-year-old boy in Boston who made a request of Brown in 1857. Would Brown, then famous as a warrior against slavery, write a letter telling what kind of boy he had been? Captain Brown had smiled broadly and said that he would, but he let almost 10 months pass before sending the letter to young Henry Stearns. Though the letter does not tell everything we might like to know, most scholars agree that it is a masterpiece of self-revelation: that the 57-year-old Brown related useful and important details about the boy he once had been:

> When he was five years old his Father moved to Ohio; then a wilderness filled with wild beasts, & Indians. . . . After getting to Ohio in 1805, he was for some time rather afraid of the Indians, & of their Rifles; but this soon wore off: & he used to hang about them quite as much as was consistent with good manners; & learned a trifle of their talk.[4]

Moving from Connecticut to Ohio was very much like leaving civilization for the frontier, but the move does not seem to have filled young John with terror. Like many young boys of that time, he was accustomed to hardship and to difficulty from an early age. What stands out is young John spending time with the Native Americans of eastern Ohio; this was probably not the norm for frontier boys, and it indicates that his family may have entertained more liberal ideas—especially about race and ethnicity—than was normally the case. Brown continued his tale:

> At eight years old, John was left a Motherless boy, which loss was complete & permanent for notwithstanding his Father again married to a sensible, intelligent, & on many accounts a very estimable woman: *yet he never adopted her in feeling:* but continued to pine after his own Mother for years.[5]

It was much more common for a young person to experience losing a parent because of the hardships during that time, but the emotional loss seems to have been severe, and in some ways Brown was never the same again. "During the war with England [the War of 1812] a circumstance occurred that in the end made him a most determined Abolitionist: [and] led him to declare, or Swear: Eternal war with slavery."[6]

Twelve-year-old John helped his father drive a herd of cattle to a U.S. Army barracks; the exact location is not given, but one suspects it was in the neighborhood of Fort Detroit, where the city of the same name later sprang up. He and his father stayed at the home of an army officer who had a young black slave, about John's age. This slave appears to have been very friendly and helpful to young John.

> *The Master* made a great pet of John: brought him to table with his first company; & friends; called their attention to every little smart thing he *said* or *did* ... while the *negro boy* (who was fully if not more than his equal) was badly clothed, poorly fed; *& lodged in cold weather.* & beaten before his eyes with Iron Shovels or any other thing that came first to hand.[7]

As appalling as this sounds, it was very likely true. There were "good" masters and "bad" ones, and this U.S. Army officer appears to have been one of the latter.

> This brought John to reflect on the wretched, hopeless condition, of *Fatherless & Motherless* slave children: for such children have neither Fathers or Mothers to protect, & provide for them. He would sometimes raise the question: is God their Father?[8]

Still grieving over the loss of his mother, young John came to identify with black slaves. He saw them as especially vulnerable because, even if they had mothers and fathers, those parents were unable to defend them from the abuses handed out by vindictive slave masters. Brown wrote these words in 1857, with a lack of self-consciousness that is much less common today, and his words reveal the boy, his personal pain, and the way in which he came to identify with black Americans.

Brown's autobiographical essay ends with his marriage to Dianthe Lusk in the summer of 1820. Brown was 20, and Lusk was a year or two younger. In a rather short time, Brown became the father of several children and the kind of provider that he saw as missing for African Americans. At that same time, the nation was experiencing growing pains of its own.

EXPANSION AND CONFLICT

When Brown was born, in 1800, there were 16 stars on the American flag: the original 13 states plus Vermont (which entered the Union in 1791), Kentucky (1792), and Tennessee (1796). The nation could still be described as hugging the eastern seaboard, but that condition did not remain for long.

Ohio became the seventeenth state in 1803. A number of others followed, and until 1820, there was little conflict in the nation's growth. That year, Missouri petitioned for admission as a slave state (a state that permitted slavery), and a major

In 1820, with the admission of Maine (a free state) and Missouri (a slave state) into statehood, equal representation in the Senate was maintained. On the map, the areas in yellow are slave states; the blue region represents unorganized territory; and the region in brown, purple, and dark green is free.

controversy was sparked in Washington, D.C. There were, at that time, 11 free states and 11 slave states, and to allow Missouri into the Union would throw off the geographic balance, as well as the numeric balance in the U.S. Senate and House of Representatives.

Months of wrangling followed, and toward the end of the year leading congressmen found a solution, called the Missouri Compromise. It was agreed that Missouri would enter the Union as a slave state and that Maine (which was sectioned off from Massachusetts) would come in as a free state, thus preserving the numeric balance in the U.S. Congress. Just as important, Congress voted for, and President James Monroe signed, a stipulation that slavery would never exist north of the line of 36 degrees, 30 minutes north latitude, which was Missouri's southwestern border. As difficult as the Compromise of 1820 had been, many, if not most, white Americans believed that the major problem had been solved. The nation could continue to grow in a westward direction, with free states occupying the northern tier and slave states expanding in the southern one. The nation could remain half slave and half free.

Nevertheless, conflict simmered just below the surface.

THE FIRST ABOLITIONISTS

The word *abolish* means "to end" or "to eliminate." It was the goal of the abolitionists to end or eliminate slavery. They had their work cut out for them.

Abolition was more successful in Great Britain, where slavery had never taken hold in a deep or strong way. A ruling by a British judge, in 1772, outlawed slavery on British soil, and a major humanitarian campaign led to England outlawing British participation in the slave trade in 1807. Some Americans naturally pointed to Great Britain—the country from which the United States had won its independence—and said it was shameful that it was ahead of the United States in this vital area. American abolitionists began to pick up where England's had left off.

Though a handful of Quaker (Society of Friends) groups had condemned slavery as early as the 1780s, the first major American abolitionist movement began in 1831, when William Lloyd Garrison, a Boston journalist, published a newspaper called *The Liberator*. In it he agitated unceasingly for the end of slavery. He would not fight, however, because he was a Quaker who believed in nonviolent means. Over the next few years, Garrison became the foremost spokesman for the idea of *moral suasion*, meaning that Northerners should educate, and slowly persuade, Southerners to abolish slavery on their own.

As a result of his outspokenness, Garrison was dragged through the streets of Boston by an angry mob and nearly lynched in 1835. The same thing also happened to a number of other Northern newspapermen, but it was in the West that mob violence did its worst. In the summer of 1837, a mob confronted, and then killed, the abolitionist newspaperman Elijah P. Lovejoy in Illinois.

Upon hearing of Lovejoy's death, 37-year-old John Brown stood up in a church and swore eternal war against slavery.

MIDDLE-AGED BROWN

Brown enjoyed being a family man. He and Dianthe would have seven children, beginning a year after they were married with John Jr., until 1832. Brown would experience heartache, losing two children and Dianthe, who died in 1832.

Until his mid-thirties, Brown was a reasonably successful farmer and tanner—skills he had learned from his hardworking father. Soon after the death of his wife, Brown sought to make some easy money in an opportunity that was popular during that time: speculation in land. The price of land, especially on the frontier, had steadily increased for more than a dozen years, and Brown thought that he was entering the speculation business at just the right time. Instead, he entered the land market shortly before the Panic of 1837, one of the greatest economic downturns in American history.

Brown became one of thousands of Americans saddled with debt. The decline in his personal fortunes mirrored the state of the nation, but it also came at a particularly bad time: Brown had married 16-year-old Mary Ann Day on June 14, 1833, and his tenth child had just been born. John and Mary eventually would have 13 children, in addition to the 7 children from his first marriage. So, in the same year that Brown swore eternal war against slavery, he was engaged in a war closer to home, trying to put food on the table. In many ways, this personal battle would never end; Brown would always be just a few

After the death of his first wife, Dianthe, Brown married Mary Ann Day. Mary Ann and John would eventually have 13 children, in addition to the 7 he had with Dianthe. Mary Ann is pictured here with two of their daughters.

steps ahead of the sheriff and a few weeks away from debtor's jail for the rest of his life.

THE PLAN

Sometime in the mid-1840s, Brown formed a kernel of the idea of what later became his Harpers Ferry raid. At the time, it was only a thought or a dream that he confided to just a few people, but over the years this idea would grow into an obsession. One of the first people he told outside of his family was the abolitionist Frederick Douglass.

Born into slavery in Maryland in 1818, Douglass escaped around the age of 20 and made his way north to New Bedford,

Massachusetts. He earned a modest living as a day laborer until some of the abolitionist societies in Massachusetts realized that, in Douglass, they had a better spokesman for their cause than any white person. Strong, handsome, and charismatic, Douglass became a regular speaker at abolitionist group meetings. In 1847, he met Brown in Springfield, Massachusetts.

Brown had moved with three of his sons to Springfield, where he enjoyed modest success as a dealer in sheep's wool. His wife, Mary, joined him in 1846, and the Browns lived in a section of Springfield that had a number of free blacks. Just as he had mixed easily with Native Americans in youth, Brown moved easily among African Americans in middle age. Douglass visited Brown at his wool shop, then went to Brown's house for dinner. Douglass commented, "My welcome was all that I could have asked. Every member of the family, young and old, seemed glad to see me, and I was made much at home in a very short while."[9]

Douglass was neither the first nor the last visitor to remark on the open spirit of the Brown family. It seemed to be a family rule that visitors—whether black or white—were treated with respect and that they received all of the family's attention. After a meal, which Douglass described as spartan (meaning "simple" or "frugal"), Brown explained his plan for liberating the Southern slaves. As Douglass related:

> He called my attention to a map of the United States, and pointed out to me the far-reaching Alleghenics, which stretch away from the borders of New York into the Southern States. "These mountains," he said, "are the basis of my plan. God has given the strength of the hills to freedom; they were placed here for the emancipation of the negro race; they are full of natural forts, where one man for defense will be equal to a hundred for attack."[10]

Brown laid out his plan to develop a force of 50 to 100 guerrilla fighters. He would lead them into the mountains and make sudden, surprise attacks on the slaveholding communities of Virginia and Maryland. The raiders and the slaves whom they freed would quickly escape back into the mountains, where they would use the natural defenses to make themselves indestructible against Southern assaults. Eventually, Brown asserted, the slaveholders of Virginia and Maryland would grow so discouraged that they would either free their slaves or sell them into the Deep South, meaning Georgia, Alabama, and Tennessee. In either case, the northernmost part of the South would be rid of slavery.

Douglass admired the bold spirit of the plan, but he pointed out what he thought were important defects. First, the raiders might be tracked down and killed. Second, might it not be better to apply moral suasion—to persuade Southern slaveholders to relinquish their property voluntarily? Douglass recalled: "When I suggested that we might convert the slaveholders, he became much excited, and said that could never be, 'he knew their proud hearts and that they would never be induced to give up their slaves, until they felt a big stick about their heads.'"[11]

As for the idea of being hunted down, Brown believed it was unlikely, but he said he had but one life to lose and that he could not think of a better cause in which to lose it. Douglass left the next day, deeply impressed by Brown's passion and spirit, but still unsure about the plan itself.

Douglass and Brown became fast and firm friends, but a decade and more passed before Brown was able to put his plan into action.

The Bleeding
Prairie

Beginning in the 1850s, the Kansas Territory became known as "Bleeding Kansas." The territory "bled" during the 1850s because of the violent contest between those who wanted to make it a free state and those who wished to make it an extension of the slaveholding South.

THE COMPROMISE OF 1850

In the winter of 1849–1850, California applied for admission to the Union. Thanks to the Gold Rush of 1848, California had experienced the fastest growth yet seen by a U.S. territory, and it had the mandatory number of souls to ask for statehood. By a rather close vote, Californians voted to come in as a free state, one where slavery was prohibited.

The application caused a firestorm in Washington, D.C. Ever since the Missouri Compromise of 1820, there had been

The Fugitive Slave Law of 1850 forced Northerners to aid in the capture of runaway slaves without due process of law and prohibited anyone from aiding in blocking their recovery. This law had the opposite of its intended effect, causing an increase in abolitionist activity. This painting shows four runaways attempting to escape slave catchers.

an equal number of free states and slave states. California was such a large state, however, that its admission would alter that balance.

In the spring of 1850, several leading members of the U.S. Senate delivered their last great speeches on this matter. John C. Calhoun of South Carolina, who was too sick to stand, asked a colleague, Senator James Mason of Virginia, to deliver his speech. In his address, Calhoun claimed that the Southern slaveholding states must have room in which to expand. If the Northern states did not permit the expansion of slavery, then the Southern ones would know what to do (a not too veiled

CRACKDOWN ON RUNAWAYS

> No person held to service or labor in one State, under the laws thereof, escaping into another, shall, in consequence of any law or regulation therein, be discharged from such service or labor, but shall be delivered up on claim of the party to whom such service or labor may be due.*

This is from the U.S. Constitution. Written in 1787, it does not use the word slave.

> That any person who shall knowingly and willingly obstruct, hinder, or prevent such claimant, his agent or attorney, or any person or persons lawfully assisting him, or them, from arresting such a fugitive from service or labor . . . or shall harbor or conceal such fugitive . . . be subject to a fine not exceeding one thousand dollars, and imprisonment not exceeding six months.**

This is from the Fugitive Slave Act of 1850, written as part of the Compromise of 1850. The language is much stronger. Today, $1,000 may not seem overwhelming, but in 1850, the average laborer made perhaps half that much a year.

Between 1787, when the Constitution was written, and 1850, when the great Compromise was enacted, thousands of black slaves had run away. Many had been caught and returned for punishment and further labor, but many others had made their way to freedom. The Fugitive Slave Act of 1850 was written to prevent that from continuing and to establish serious penalties for Northerners who assisted runaways.

---

*Our Documents: 100 Milestone Documents from the National Archives. New York: Oxford University Press, 2003, p. 34.
**Eighteenth Annual Report Presented to the Massachusetts Anti-Slavery Society, reprint 1970. Negro Universities Press, pp. 105–106.

threat of secession, or separation, from the Union). Henry Clay of Kentucky, who had been one of the strongest voices for compromise throughout his long career, called for yet another, one that included bringing California in as a free state. Daniel Webster of Massachusetts disappointed his many abolitionist constituents by, likewise, arguing for expansion. After several months of wrangling, the U.S. Congress passed a set of bills that formed the Compromise of 1850. Under its provisions:

☆ California entered the Union as a free state
☆ The slave trade—though not slavery itself—was banned in the District of Columbia
☆ The areas that later became New Mexico, Arizona, and Utah would eventually be formed into states, with the people there having the choice of whether to enter as slave or free; and
☆ A new, much-stronger Fugitive Slave Act was enacted.

Although a few discordant voices warned of trouble in the future, most Americans were delighted by the compromise, which, they felt, had the potential to settle the slave-or-free question for decades to come. They failed to realize the significance of the Fugitive Slave Act, which now required Northern sheriffs and constables—on penalty of heavy fines and possible imprisonment—to assist slave catchers in the Northern states. Penalties were imposed upon anyone who did not enforce the law, including individuals who aided black people to escape.

John Brown was not deceived.

THE LEAGUE OF GILEADITES

By 1850, Brown had moved his large family from Springfield, Massachusetts, to North Elba, New York, where he had been offered a large tract of land on very easy credit terms. The offer came from Gerrit Smith, a wealthy abolitionist and politician. Even as he moved his family to the Adirondack Mountains in New York, Brown remained concerned about the free black community of Springfield. In the winter of 1851, he established the League of Gileadites, an organization that worked to protect escaped slaves from slave catchers, and wrote a declaration of intent for those who intended to resist slave catchers:

> Nothing so charms the American people as personal bravery.... Colored people have ten times the number of fast friends among the whites than they suppose, and would have ten times the number they have now were they but half as much in earnest to secure their dearest rights as they are to ape the follies and extravagances of their white neighbors, and to indulge in idle show, in ease, and in luxury.[1]

Some African-American readers must have smiled at these words. They knew very little about "follies" and "extravagances," but in Brown at least, African Americans met a white man who seemed as keen on their people's freedom as they were themselves. Brown continued:

> Should one of your number be arrested, you must collect together as quickly as possible.... Let no able-bodied man appear on the ground unequipped.... Your plan must be known only to yourself, and with the understanding that all traitors must die, wherever caught and proven to be guilty. "Whosoever is fearful or afraid, let him return and part early from Mount Gilead" (Book of Judges, vii. 3: Deuteronomy xx.8).[2]

This was the usual John Brown. He saw himself as a modern-day Moses or Joshua, appointed by God to lead black Americans out of slavery. Brown did not have an opportunity to lead the

The mural *Tragic Prelude*, which hangs in the east wing of the Kansas statehouse, portrays John Brown as many Southerners saw him—as a Bible-wielding, gun-toting religious fanatic. Over the century and a half that followed, other images of John Brown emerged, leading to a discussion of whether he was a saint, a fanatic, or a terrorist.

Gileadites in action before he completed the move to North Elba, New York, but the record indicates that no black person, once having made her or his way to Springfield, was ever taken from there by a slave catcher. The same could not be said of Boston.

ANTHONY BURNS

In the spring of 1854, an escaped slave named Anthony Burns was apprehended in Boston. The slave catcher, and the Boston police who assisted him, took Burns to the Boston jail and waited for a ship to take him back to slavery in Virginia.

Bostonians had long been a revolutionary people. In the 1760s, their city had been the first to resist British taxes, and the famed battles of Lexington and Concord had been fought just 20 miles (32 kilometers) away. Embarrassed by the thought that they were a lesser generation than their ancestors, abolitionist Bostonians rallied to defend Burns.

When the slave catcher and his police escort tried to take Burns to the waterfront, they found more than 1,000 abolitionists, some with posters and signs and others with concealed weapons. Thinking that the commotion would quiet down, the slave catcher determined to wait, but while he did, a handful of Bostonians broke into the jail. They did not succeed in rescuing Burns, but managed to kill a constable. This death turned many Bostonians against the abolitionist movement, but it still required about 1,500 regular U.S. Army soldiers and 500 Boston militiamen to get Burns down to the ship. (A Boston abolitionist group later purchased Burns's freedom, and he ended his days as a teacher in Canada.)

By a remarkable coincidence, the passage of legislation that furthered the conflict between slavery and freedom was passed in the same week that Burns was taken.

KANSAS-NEBRASKA ACT

In the winter of 1854, Senator Stephen A. Douglas of Illinois (he and Abraham Lincoln later squared off in the famous Lincoln-Douglas debates) introduced the Kansas-Nebraska Act to the U.S. Congress. Personally indifferent to slavery, Senator Douglas wanted to organize Kansas and Nebraska as new territories, in which the residents could decide whether to come into the Union as slave or free states. His major goal was to ensure territorial status, as a necessary first step toward statehood. Introducing the Kansas-Nebraska Act, however, had the effect of throwing Congress and the nation into another great debate over slavery.

As in 1850, there were more voices for compromise than for a fight between the different sections. In May 1854, Congress passed the Kansas-Nebraska Act. Almost immediately, Northern and Southern groups began to move to these territories with the intention of securing them for slavery or for freedom.

At this time, Brown was in Ohio, visiting several of his sons. In August, he wrote to his son John Jr. back home in North Elba:

> If you or any of my family are disposed to go to Kansas or Nebraska, with a view to help defeat Satan and his legions in that direction, I have not a word to say; *but* I feel committed to operate in another part of the field. If I were not so committed, I would be on my way this fall.[3]

Brown was referring to slavery as "Satan"; as to "another part of the field," this probably meant that Brown was still intent on his idea of establishing a base in the Appalachian Mountains, from which to harass the slave owners of Virginia and Maryland. But that situation was not yet ripe, and Brown would soon be called to Kansas.

THE TERRITORY

In the summer of 1855, Brown received a letter from four of his sons. John Jr., Frederick, Salmon, and Owen had all moved to the Kansas Territory some months earlier. They had founded a place they called Brown's Station, not far from the home of Brown's half-sister, who had moved to Kansas ahead of them. The sons reported on the battle between the forces of slavery and those of freedom.

The Kansas Territory was practically in a state of war. A large group of Missourians, called the Border Ruffians, crossed the border into Kansas each time there was a territorial election. Not only did they intimidate Kansans, but the Border Ruffians voted illegally, creating what the Browns called the Bogus Legislature at Topeka. Opposed to them were the "Free Staters," who intended to keep slavery out of Kansas. Finally, there were a few, like the Brown brothers, who were both Free Staters and abolitionists.

The letter from his sons asked Brown to come to Kansas, bringing plenty of guns with him. He was on his way in a matter of hours. Along the way, Brown received support and encouragement from Northern abolitionists. In Ohio, for example, he was given the gift of a number of surplus U.S. Army broadswords; these weapons were meant to slash and kill, rather than parry and thrust. Brown wisely kept them under tarps in the wagon on the long way to Kansas.

"OLD" BROWN

By the time he arrived in Kansas in October 1855, John Brown had begun to call himself "Old Brown." This referred to his position as the family patriarch. From his two wives (Dianthe Lusk and Mary Day), Brown had 20 children, though several had died from accidents or disease. He was an admired leader, an old man in the best sense of the word.

When he arrived at Brown's Station, about 50 miles (80 kilometers) south of the Free State town of Lawrence, Kansas, Brown found that his sons were very ill. Almost all of them had the ague (fever and chills) and were living in a combination of tents and lean-tos. Brown soon rectified the situation. Within three weeks, he had built a rough cabin, and he soon had his sons well enough to work on another. Being "old" had not diminished his capacity for work

At the same time, Brown took it upon himself to organize a militia company. He and his sons had a handful of Free State neighbors, but there were plenty of pro-slavery men in the neighborhood. Brown created a 20-man company of volunteers ranging in age from 19 to 55, with himself as captain. Soon, he was known as "Captain" John Brown as well as "Old" Brown.

A crisis at the beginning of December 1855 required Brown to muster his militia and march to Lawrence, which was threatened by a group of Border Ruffians. Thanks to the onset of winter (this was called the "Siberian" winter of 1855–1856), there was no fighting that season, but Brown praised his militia members, saying they were a group of well-behaved, self-directed men "sustaining the character of the Revolutionary Fathers."[4]

The real test came in the spring.

POTTAWATOMIE

On May 21, 1856, hundreds of Border Ruffians from Missouri sacked the town of Lawrence. The Free State men laid down their arms and watched helplessly as the Border Ruffians burned the town hotel and threw the printing press of the Free State newspaper into a nearby river.

Brown and his militia marched from the little town of Osawatomie, but they arrived too late. From a hillside, several miles south, they watched the flames over Lawrence. Just as they were about to retire, Brown and his men learned of a brutal attack on Senator Charles Sumner of Massachusetts.

BROOKS VERSUS SUMNER

Sumner had taken up the standard once held by Daniel Webster, who had painfully disappointed his constituents by voting for the Compromise of 1850. Webster was now dead, and Sumner was the new darling of the Northern abolitionists.

On May 20, 1856, Sumner gave an impassioned speech entitled "The Crime Against Kansas." Sumner justly condemned the Border Ruffians' incursions into Kansas, but he went too far when he portrayed a Southern colleague, Senator Andrew Butler of South Carolina, as having slavery as his mistress. Butler was not on hand to defend himself, and the necessity of doing so passed to his nephew, Preston Brooks, a member of the U.S. House of Representatives.

Brooks entered the Senate chamber late in the afternoon of May 21. He found Sumner at his desk and a handful of other people scattered about the room. Even today, it remains uncertain whether Brooks challenged his opponent or simply began to strike him, but in either case, the Southern representative

SOUTHERN CHIVALRY — ARGUMENT versus CLUB'S.

Senator Charles Sumner became a martyr for the anti-slavery cause the day Congressman Preston Brooks entered the Senate chamber and proceeded to beat Sumner with his cane. This act caused further rifts between the North and South, with Northerners expressing outrage and Southerners supporting Brooks's act.

used a cane and began to beat the Northern senator. Sumner tried to rise, but his chair and desk were bolted to the floor. In a short period of time, Sumner fell on the floor, unconscious and bleeding profusely. Brooks continued to beat him until he broke his cane, then straightened his shoulders and walked out of the Senate chamber. He was never arrested or prosecuted.

Sumner spent the next three years recovering from the attack. He suffered from head trauma, nightmares, severe headaches, and what is now known as post-traumatic stress disorder. During that time, the Commonwealth of Massachusetts purposely left his Senate chair empty, as a symbol of free speech and resistance to slavery. As a consequence of the assault, senators and representatives—North and South alike—often took concealed weapons to Congress for the next few years.

THE MASSACRE

The advent of the telegraph, just a few years before, allowed Brown and other Kansans to learn the news quickly. Coupled with the Sack of Lawrence, this brutal attack against a Northern senator propelled Brown into action.

On the evening of May 24, 1856, Brown led three of his sons and a handful of their friends to a cabin along Pottawatomie Creek. The Doyle family was known for its pro-slavery sentiments, and some of the Doyles had made threats against some of the Browns. John Brown went straight to their door, where, at gunpoint, he ordered James Doyle and two of his sons to come outside (the 16-year-old was allowed to stay with his mother). Mrs. Doyle later commented that Brown had "an eye like a snake."[5]

Brown watched as his men used broadswords to kill the Doyles, splitting open their heads and cutting off their arms. Brown then put a bullet into the head of James Doyle. Brown's party entered another cabin and hauled out two other pro-slavery men. By the time dawn came, Brown and his fellows had executed five men in cold blood. Later, Brown claimed that five Free State men had been murdered over the previous month and that blood was necessary to answer blood.

MEETING JAMES REDPATH

About 10 days later, Brown made the acquaintance of 24-year-old James Redpath, a Scottish journalist. Redpath had immigrated to New York and then moved to Kansas in search of a good story, and he found one in Captain John Brown, as he usually called him. Redpath recalled their first meeting:

> Brown himself stood near the fire, with his shirt-sleeves rolled up, and a large piece of pork in his hands. He was

cooking a pig. He was poorly clad, and his toes protruded from his boots. The old man received me with great cordiality, and the little band gathered about me.[6]

Redpath inquired about the massacre at Pottawatomie, but he was not eager to bring down the reputation of this Free State leader. Redpath concentrated, instead, on the heroic qualities of Brown and his men. Noting that Brown would not allow any profanity to be used, Redpath commented on the old man's attitude:

> It was at this time that the old man said to me: "I would rather have the small-pox, yellow fever, and cholera all together in my camp, than a man without principles. It is a mistake sir," he continued, "that our people make, when they think that bullies are the best fighters, or that they are the men fit to oppose these Southerners. Give me men of good principles, God-fearing men; men who respect themselves; and with a dozen of them, I will oppose any hundred such men as these Buford ruffians.[7]

He was about to demonstrate the truth in these words.

The Concord
Connection

Osawatomie, Kansas, is a long way from Concord, Massachusetts, but John Brown and the handful of followers he gathered in the summer of 1856 saw a strong connection between the two places. Like many Americans of his time, Brown believed the American Revolution of 1775 had been a very good thing—in some ways the best to happen in recent human history—but he also saw it as incomplete. What the embattled farmers of Lexington and Concord had begun in April 1775, he and others intended to finish, sometime in the near future.

BATTLE OF BLACK JACK

Pro-slavery forces had gone on a manhunt, searching the countryside for the Pottawatomie killers. Brown hid in the woods and evaded capture. Captain Henry C. Pate of Virginia and his men had been called on to capture Brown and headed to the town of Osawatomie, near the border of Brown's Station. Pate found two of Brown's sons—John Jr. and Jason, who had not been involved in the massacre—and they were abducted and severely beaten. On May 31, the two Brown boys were marched in irons to the Santa Fe Trail near Hickory Point and made camp on a small branch called Black Jack.

As soon as the elder Brown heard of his sons' capture, he was determined to rescue them. As he traveled through the woods, he watched for the enemy's camp. Two scouts who had been helping Brown brought the news of the location of Pate's camp on the Black Jack, some miles away. On June 2, Brown and about 20 men went on the hunt for Pate. This time it was an even fight. Both sides had rifles, muskets, and daggers.

Brown commenced the attack, even though he was outnumbered by two-to-one. The Missourians, led by Pate, defended a position that included four wagons, drawn up in an excellent posture for defense. All morning, rifle fire ricocheted between the two sides, with the Free State men generally getting the best of their pro-slavery adversaries. Brown lost several men to rifle fire and some of the others were ready to desert; then it became apparent that the Missourians were in worse shape. By twos, and sometimes threes, the Missourians ran off, leaving their commander to arrange a truce.

Not knowing the slender size of his opponent's force, Pate came out to negotiate for terms, only to be told that his surrender must be complete and unconditional. Minutes later, Pate and his men were prisoners. Brown had his first legitimate battle victory (what he did at Pottawatomie can only be called a massacre).

Free State men and abolitionists in the Kansas Territory were elated to hear of Brown's victory. During the past two years, the idea had spread that any good Southern man (meaning pro-slavery person) could whip any two Northern men (meaning Free Staters). Brown did much to rebuff that notion.

The controversy over slavery in Kansas Territory rocked the nation, causing Free-Staters and Border Ruffians to fight it out to the bloody end. Both
sides showed no mercy, committing atrocities against citizens who did not
support their cause. Pictured are Free-State prisoners near Lecompton,
Kansas Territory, including John Brown Jr. *(second from left)*.

BATTLE OF OSAWATOMIE

Late that summer, the Border Ruffians struck again. This
time, they crossed the border very near Brown's Station, and
attacked the little town of Osawatomie (with a population of
about 200).

Brown knew the Ruffians were coming, and he waited for
them with about 30 volunteers. Moments before the battle

began, he learned that a minister in the pro-slavery forces had struck down and killed his son Frederick, who was not part of Brown's military command at the time. Learning of his son's death prompted Brown to fight even harder. He and his 30 men were able to hold off about 10 times their number of pro-slavery men for an hour or two, making the Battle of Osawatomie a standoff, rather than a Southern victory. The journalist James Redpath was not there on the day of the battle, but he later noted: "When the writer visited the site, many months after this event, the wood still bore the marks of that glorious conflict."[1]

Soon after the Battle of Osawatomie, John Brown left the Kansas Territory.

THE SECRET SIX

Brown first went back to North Elba, New York, for a joyful reunion with his wife, whom he had not seen in 16 months. Their baby girl had turned into a three-year-old during his absence.

Brown spent only a week or two at home before heading to eastern Massachusetts, where he hoped to win the support and financial backing of men associated with the Kansas cause. His first stop was in Boston, where he met Franklin Sanborn, secretary of the Massachusetts Emigrant Aid Society. Brown must have made a good impression, for within the next six weeks he met nearly all the men who later called themselves the "Secret Six." They were:

☆ Theodore Parker, a Boston minister who had been a passionate abolitionist for about a decade.

☆ Thomas Wentworth Higginson, a Worcester, Massachusetts, minister who had led the Bostonians who tried to break Anthony Burns from jail in 1854.

☆ George Luther Stearns, a wealthy Boston businessman, whose Medford estate became the chief meeting ground for the conspirators.

Shown are replicas of the pikes John Brown hoped to use after the slave uprising. Brown had contracted 1,500 pikes from a Connecticut blacksmith for his abolitionist army but they were never used. Today, similar pikes hang on display at Harpers Ferry National Historical Park in Harpers Ferry, West Virginia.

☆ Samuel Gridley Howe, a teacher of the blind, whose wife would play a major role in furthering John Brown's legend.
☆ Franklin Sanborn, the youngest of the six.
☆ Gerrit Smith, abolitionist, politician, and philanthropist, of upstate New York.

Unlike Brown, the Secret Six had lived lives of privilege. Nevertheless, they had something else that bound them together. They identified with the American Revolution, and they also believed that a second part, or act, was necessary to complete the promise of that first attempt. For example, the Reverend Theodore Parker was the grandson of Captain John Parker, who, during the American Revolution, had led

DRED SCOTT V. SANDFORD

Chief Justice Roger Taney delivered the Supreme Court's ruling in this historic case on March 7, 1857:

> The question before us, is whether the class of persons [blacks] described in the plea of abatement compose a portion of this people [Americans], and are constituent members of this sovereignty? We think they are not and that they are not included, and were not intended to be included, under the word "citizens" in the Constitution, and can therefore claim none of the rights and privileges which that instrument provides for and secures to citizens of the United States.*

Today, we would find this preposterous. How could the Supreme Court say that people of any creed, color, or background were not citizens? Taney quoted Thomas Jefferson's famous words from the Declaration of Independence, "all men are created equal," and went on to say:

> The general words above quoted would seem to embrace the whole human family, and if they were used in a similar instrument at this day would be so understood. But It is too clear for dispute, that the enslaved African race were not intended to be included, and formed no part of the people who framed and adopted this declaration. . . . The court is of the opinion, that, upon the facts stated in the plea In abatement, Dred Scott was not a citizen of Missouri within the meaning of the Constitution of the United States, and not entitled as such to sue in its courts."**

(continues)

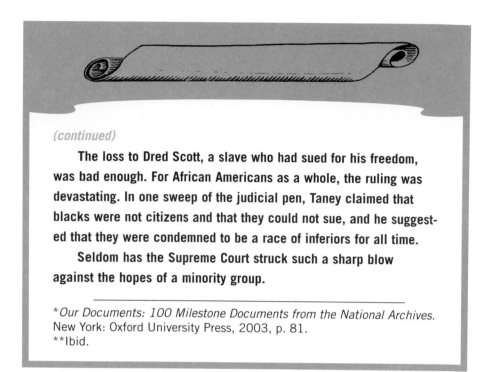

(continued)

The loss to Dred Scott, a slave who had sued for his freedom, was bad enough. For African Americans as a whole, the ruling was devastating. In one sweep of the judicial pen, Taney claimed that blacks were not citizens and that they could not sue, and he suggested that they were condemned to be a race of inferiors for all time.

Seldom has the Supreme Court struck such a sharp blow against the hopes of a minority group.

*Our Documents: 100 Milestone Documents from the National Archives. New York: Oxford University Press, 2003, p. 81.
**Ibid.

the Minutemen on Lexington Green in April 1775. Samuel Gridley Howe's father had participated in the Boston Tea Party. Howe himself had gone to Greece in 1825 to join in the Greek Revolution against the Ottoman Turks. What these very different men shared was a belief that the American Revolution must be completed. Brown seemed like the right kind of incendiary to bring about that kind of change.

The two most prominent intellectual leaders of the day did not join the movement, or render financial support, but Brown impressed them, too. The first time Brown went to Concord, Massachusetts, to lecture, essayist and poet Ralph Waldo Emerson invited him to spend the night at his house. On a second occasion, Brown had tea with Henry David Thoreau, the author of *Walden; or Life in the Woods*, a book about independence and spiritual discovery.

Connection with the Concord intellectuals gave Brown something he had never had before—a major audience—and in March he addressed the Massachusetts legislature, asking for help with his work in Kansas. Brown held up a pair of chains, which he said were the ones that had imprisoned his son John Jr. He spoke passionately but did not win any converts in the legislature, which had its mind on plenty of other matters.

Brown made a major move toward his plan when he contracted with a Connecticut blacksmith to furnish 1,500 pikes for a future army of freed slaves. Brown reasoned that newly freed slaves would be unfamiliar with firearms and that pikes would make weapons that were easier to use. Brown did not collect all the pikes for another two years.

Even if Brown did not capture Emerson's and Thoreau's complete support and the men of the Secret Six had been inclined to dismiss him as too radical for their tastes, the Supreme Court ruling in *Dred Scott v. Sandford* would change their opinion.

NEW YORK

Brown pushed on to New York City, which he found much less to his liking. There were a few prominent pastors who quietly supported his work, but the city, as a whole, was much less abolitionist-minded than Boston. Before long, Brown was back in North Elba.

Brown's trip east had been a success in many ways. He had come across as a man of reason and integrity, and the high-minded Concord intellectuals had taken him in. Still Brown was disappointed by the lack of financial support, and when potential backers asked him how he would use their money, he turned very frosty indeed. Old Brown was not to be questioned on such matters. In the late summer of 1857, Brown wrote an open letter to his critics, suggesting that they were cowards at a time when action was called for. He called it "Old Brown's Farewell."

Brown's supporters liked his idea of establishing a base in the Appalachian Mountains (he had not revealed his plans about

Harpers Ferry), but they wanted him to accomplish more in the Kansas Territory to smooth the way to that greater enterprise.

KANSAS AND IOWA

By the time he arrived on the Iowa-Kansas border in the summer of 1857, Brown found that tensions within the Kansas Territory were greatly reduced. There had been no major outbreak of lawlessness that year, and men on both sides, Free State and pro-slavery alike, were becoming reconciled to the idea that Kansas would eventually become a free state.

Brown spent several months in Iowa, coordinating activities with a handful of Quakers from the town of Tabor. He did not, of course, tell them all his plans, but he asked them to house 200 Sharps rifles for the time being: These guns had been provided by the Massachusetts Emigrant Aid Society. During the autumn of 1857, Brown found a handful of recruits, men who professed a willingness to follow him anywhere. Two of the most important were John Cook and Aaron Stevens. They could hardly have been more different. The amiable, reserved, 23-year-old Cook was a lanky man with a shock of blond hair, while Stevens, dark-haired and as strong as an ox, was a former U.S. Army corporal who had deserted and suffered severe consequences. What drew them to Brown was the same combination of cheerfulness and willpower that he had used to win over the Secret Six. There is little doubt that Brown was clever and charming, able to win the hearts of men as different as Emerson and Thoreau, and Cook and Stevens.

THE NEW CONSTITUTION

Brown left Iowa toward the end of 1857 and spent the first two months of the new year at the home of Frederick Douglass in Rochester, New York. Eleven years had passed since their first meeting, but their relationship was as strong, and as conflicted, as ever. Brown continued to press Douglass for a commitment in favor of the raid on the armory at Harpers Ferry, while Douglass continued to believe that newspapers and books could apply moral suasion to the Southern slaveholders. Though he did not win Douglass over, Brown put the two months to good use. He wrote a provisional constitution that would create a new government for the state of his invasion, which he took to a convention in May in Chatham Township, in the province of Ontario, Canada. One third of Chatham's 6,000 residents were fugitive slaves, and Brown conveyed his plan to make Kansas, rather than Canada, the end of the Underground Railroad. The convention assembled 34 blacks and 12 whites to adopt Brown's provisional constitution. In the preamble, Brown lost no time in getting to the heart of the matter:

> Whereas slavery, throughout its entire existence in the United States, is none other than a most barbaric, unprovoked, and unjustifiable war of one portion of its citizens upon another portion—the only conditions of which are perpetual imprisonment and hopeless servitude or absolute extermination—in utter disregard and violation of those external and self-evident truths set forth in our Declaration of Independence.[2]

While the U.S. Constitution of 1787 had not even mentioned the words *slave* or *slavery*, Brown used the latter term as the second word of his preamble. Quickly, he went on to say:

> Therefore we, citizens of the United States, and the oppressed people who, by a recent decision of the Supreme Court, are declared to have no rights which the white man is bound to respect, together with all other people degraded by the laws thereof, do, for the time being, ordain and establish for ourselves the following Provisional Constitution and Ordinances.[3]

Brown was elected commander in chief, and he named a secretary of war, secretary of state, interim president, and vice president. Although nearly all of the attendees signed Brown's constitution, very few joined his cause. Many historians have poked fun at Brown over the decades, asking how one man with a handful of followers thought he could create, much less establish, a new constitution for a country that had had one for the past 70 years. That type of ridicule, though, serves to obscure the important work Brown had accomplished. Almost alone, among the white abolitionists of his time, Brown foresaw a new republic, one in which all men and all women would be equal participants. Given that the learned chief justice of the Supreme Court had recently ruled in completely the opposite way, it was no small feat for Brown to put forth his new set of ideas.

Not all blacks knew of Brown, and of those who knew him, not all liked him. But most who knew him came to recognize that Brown was a very different type of white person. Here was a white man, raised on the frontier, who had become friendly with Native Americans and grown to manhood in a republic that despised blacks, without adopting that attitude himself. There may have been other fair-minded white men like Brown, but history shows few of them to us.

Good Abolitionist Horses

In the spring of 1858, Brown felt ready to start his "mill," by which he meant the invasion of northern Virginia. But treachery within his ranks meant he had to wait a year and more.

Colonel Hugh Forbes was English by birth and had lived in Italy for a number of years. He had served in the Italian revolutionary forces in 1848 (their effort failed), and later he wrote a manual, *The Patriotic Volunteer*. In 1857, Brown had recruited Forbes as a military leader for the planned Virginia invasion. Forbes, however, was dissatisfied with the money he received and turned on Brown. By 1858, he had informed several leading American politicians, including Senator Henry Wilson of Massachusetts, of Brown's desire to take over the federal arsenal at Harpers Ferry. When they learned of this betrayal, the Secret Six—Samuel Gridley Howe, Theodore Parker, Gerrit Smith,

Thomas Wentworth Higginson, George Luther Stearns, and Franklin Sanborn—told Brown he must wait until the times were more promising. Brown reluctantly agreed, and by the summer of 1858, he was back in the Kansas Territory. This time, he found plenty of work to do.

ANOTHER MASSACRE

In May 1858, a pro-slavery man named Charles Hamilton committed an outrage at least as bad as what Brown had done at Pottawatomie Creek. Hamilton and a group of Border Ruffians captured 11 Free State men, forced them into a ravine near the Kansas-Missouri border, and casually shot them from a distance. Five were immediately killed, but several survived to tell the grisly tale. Suddenly, it seemed as if the Kansas Territory was going to "bleed" yet again.

Brown and a small group of followers reached the territory just days after the massacre. Brown took no immediate action; he almost seemed to relish the slow days of summer. On one occasion that summer, he had a chance to kill the pro-slavery minister who had killed his son Frederick in 1856. Despite calls from his men to take revenge, Brown refused. Brown said that he acted from principle and that anyone who rode with him must do the same. But for all the lofty rhetoric, Brown was eager to find a chance to strike back.

SLAVE STEALING

In the middle of December 1858, one of Brown's men had a conversation with an anxious black slave, who had stolen across the Kansas-Missouri line. The man was afraid that his master was about to split up his family by selling family members away. This was the event that sprang Brown into action.

Though he had suffered badly from malarial fever during the summer and autumn, Brown seemed recovered, and on the night of December 21, he and about 20 men crossed the

Missouri line. They first went to where the black slave lived; the house had several white occupants and four other slaves: by threatening to smoke them out, Brown won the surrender of the whites and the liberation of the blacks. He freed another five slaves from a nearby residence. Aaron Stevens, meanwhile, led another group of Brown's men to a third house, where, unfortunately, Stevens shot and killed the owner (the memory of that night haunted Stevens for the rest of his life). One slave was freed there, for a total of 11.

Moving swiftly, Brown, Stevens, and their men crossed the border and were soon back in Kansas Territory. They took the freed slaves to a hidden location and laid low, hoping that the storm of controversy would blow over. It did not.

Angry and frightened, slaveholding Missourians called for Brown's head. Even the territorial governor of Kansas put a bounty on it. President James Buchanan did the same, but none of this seemed to daunt Brown, who had become the hero of Free State Kansans. Here was a Northern man who could meet and beat Southerners at their own game of border-crossing and intimidation. After waiting a few weeks, Brown led the 11 freed blacks on an epic journey, north through Kansas, trying to reach the border with the Nebraska Territory. For most of the distance, he managed to conceal their identity, but a few miles south of the Nebraska border the blacks were identified. A large posse of Missourians awaited Brown at the Platte River, just before the border.

Knowing the danger full well, Brown, Stevens, and the others moved straight ahead. As they came to the south side of the river, the Missourians panicked, with several men fleeing on horseback. Others were captured, and, as they later confessed, treated gently by the Old Man and his rebel crew. As for Brown, this bloodless event, called the Battle of the Spurs, cemented his reputation. He had always said that he would never be taken alive; now it was claimed he could never be defeated.

As he crossed into the Nebraska Territory, Brown may have known that this was his last sight of Kansas. His greatest achievements had all been on Kansas soil, but he wanted to carry the war against slavery into the Southern slaveholding states.

BACK EAST

Brown, Stevens, and their comrades took the 11 freed blacks all the way to Detroit, Michigan, to see them safely across the border into British Canada. By now there were 12; one of the freed women gave birth to a son she named after Brown.

From there, Brown headed back East, stopping at significant points in Ohio and New York along the way. As heroic as the past two months had been, Brown found quite a few Northerners upset with him. Some claimed that the Kansas issue had finally been settled and that Brown was making trouble there when none existed. Others applauded his freeing of the slaves but lamented that he had stolen horses and wagons from the slaveholders. To Brown, these criticisms were beside the point, slave owners had already benefited from decades of slave labor. He believed that slavery was a state of war against the slave, and that whatever reparation— in terms of property—that could be claimed was justified. In Ohio, Brown sold the "abolitionist" horses he had taken from Missouri farms and sent the $250 he received straight on to North Elba.

Gerrit Smith, and other members of the Secret Six, were generally impressed with Brown's foray into Missouri (the lone exception was Samuel Gridley Howe). They were now eager for Brown to put his "mill" into operation, meaning a raid into Northern Virginia. Brown spent a week or two with his family at North Elba, visited Concord and Boston for a second time, and by the end of June he was in southern Pennsylvania, waiting for the right moment to move on Harpers Ferry.

John Edwin Cook.

After John Brown created his provisional constitution, he disbanded his party until he was ready to call for them. The exception was Captain John Cook, who was sent to Harpers Ferry to make himself familiar with the region and its citizens, especially the slaves, and to relay information to Brown.

John Cook had been at Harpers Ferry for the past 10 months, acting as the advance guard and spy for Brown's "mill." Cook had endeared himself to many in the neighborhood, even falling for and marrying a local woman.

THE NATION IN 1859

The summer of 1859 found the nation at peace, though tensions seethed below the surface. The United States was beginning to come out of the economic depression of 1857, but there were still anxieties about the future. Southern slave-holders, in particular, felt a set of concerns about the future of tobacco (which had greatly decreased in value) and cotton (which was still holding its own). Southerners were also

THE RISE OF LINCOLN

Abraham Lincoln's frontier boyhood and hardscrabble life bore numerous comparisons to John Brown's. Both grew up in the wilderness, and both lost their mothers when they were very young. A major difference is that Brown's difficulties in life created a man with a soul of iron, while Lincoln became a man of compromise and conciliation.

Born in Kentucky in 1809, Lincoln had moved first to Indiana and then Illinois. He was very much a son of the frontier, operating a riverboat on the Illinois and Mississippi rivers and fighting in the Black Hawk War of 1832. Like Brown, Lincoln experienced his share of financial humiliation over the years; unlike Brown, Lincoln had a difficult time finding a wife, finally marrying Mary Todd in 1842. By the time of the Compromise of 1850, Lincoln was a successful lawyer, living in Springfield, Illinois.

The furor over the Kansas-Nebraska Act gave birth to the Republican Party, which took three ideas as its keywords: free land, free labor, and free men. This did not mean that Republicans were abolitionists; the great majority of Republicans believed that the best that could be accomplished was to stop the spread of concerned about the presidential election of 1860; they feared that the Republican Party, which had been formed in 1854, would introduce a "black-hearted" abolitionist on the nation. This was actually the most unlikely possibility.

THE KENNEDY FARM

Operating under the alias of "Mr. Isaac Smith," Brown arrived at Harpers Ferry on the evening of July 3, 1859. The next day,

slavery to other areas. Lincoln rose fast in the Republican Party ranks. Another frontier hero, John C. Frémont, was nominated for the presidency in 1856; he lost that year's election to Democrat James Buchanan.

By 1859, Lincoln was well known in the West but little regarded in the East. Most Northern Republicans favored nominating Senator William H. Seward of New York for president the following year. Lincoln and Seward had both contributed to the Republican Party vocabulary. In 1858, Lincoln had spoken poignantly about the nation being unable to exist "half slave and half free,"* while Seward had spoken of an irrepressible conflict between the free-labor North and the slave-labor South.

In 1859, even Lincoln's greatest admirers conceded that he was a lukewarm abolitionist, at best. The same could be said for Seward. It took the actions of someone else, another frontier boy-turned-man named John Brown, to ignite the flames of the irrepressible conflict.

---

*Abraham Lincoln, "House Divided Speech," The History Place. Available online at http://www.historyplace.com/lincoln/divided.htm.

John Brown's Residence, Kennedy Farm, Maryland Heights, just before Raid at Harpers Ferry in 1859.

COPYRIGHT 1908
by W. L ERWIN
HARPERS FERRY, W. VA.

John Brown rented the Kennedy farmhouse under the name Isaac Smith, five miles north of Harpers Ferry, in Washington County, Maryland. Here his men trained and prepared for the raid. After the raid, coverage in newspapers like *Frank Leslie's Illustrated Newspaper* further polarized the country between those who condemned Brown's actions and others who viewed him as a martyr.

he and two of his sons walked through the neighborhood, and by that evening they had rented a farm about five miles (eight kilometers) north, on the Maryland side of the Potomac River. This was the Kennedy Farm, named for a physician who had lived there.

Brown's white beard was longer than ever, and he took care—while in the neighborhood—to act the part of an elderly man. He showed kindness to neighbors, serving as a veterinarian to one woman's horses, and he walked slowly, befitting a

New York State farmer who had come south to see if he could breed cattle.

Brown had been here once before, at a time when he was looking for land. On that occasion, he remarked on the difference between Northern and Southern farmers, with his opinion very much in the former's favor. This time, he had not come to compare farming systems, but to launch an all-out assault on one of the bastions of slavery.

GATHERING THE FORCE

Brown had hoped for a force of 50 to 100 guerrilla fighters, but he was disappointed. Even men who were impressed with his speeches and actions did not join up with him. Over the days and weeks that followed, a grand total of 20 people came to join his antislavery crusade. They were: Jeremiah Anderson; Osborne Anderson; his sons Oliver, Owen, and Watson Brown; John Copeland; John Cook; Barclay Coppoc; Edwin Coppoc; Albert Hazlett; John Kagi; Lewis Leary; Will Leeman; Francis Merriam; Dangerfield Newby; Aaron Stevens; Stewart Taylor; Dauphin Thompson; Will Thompson, and Charles Tidd. Four were black (Osborne Anderson, Dangerfield Newby, Lewis Leary, and John Copeland). Brown had hoped for many more African Americans, but they did not come.

The 20 accomplices came from a variety of backgrounds. Among them were two Quakers (the Coppoc brothers), a rich man (Merriam), and a variety of others. What they shared was a burning desire to free the slaves.

The connection point for the conspirators—and the way from free state Pennsylvania to slave state Maryland—was Chambersburg, Pennsylvania. Brown had his mail delivered there during the summer, and he made numerous trips from the Kennedy Farm to Chambersburg, usually under the cover of night. By late summer, Brown had given up on recruiting more men for the expedition, but he wanted a co-leader, someone to inspire the enslaved blacks of Maryland and Virginia. He wanted Frederick Douglass.

Although they had kept in touch and had even visited together the previous year, a dozen years had passed since Brown first confided his overall plan to Douglass. From the beginning, Douglass had viewed it as a noble, but madcap, scheme. Now, in the heat of August, Douglass went to southern Pennsylvania to meet secretly with Brown (he went under the guise of giving an abolitionist speech in Chambersburg).

Brown and two followers went north to Pennsylvania for the secret meeting. The person Brown most wanted to join the assault was proving reluctant. Douglass later recalled the circumstances of the meeting:

> His face wore an anxious expression, and he was much worn by thought and exposure. I felt that I was on a dangerous mission, and was as little desirous of discovery as himself, though no reward had been offered for me.[1]

There had been a price on Brown's head ever since his invasion into Missouri nine months earlier. As they sat among the rocks of a stone quarry, Brown discussed his plan with Douglass. Though Brown had often spoken of the mountains and their use to the freed blacks, he had never been so explicit about Harpers Ferry and attacking the federal arsenal. This made Douglass very nervous, and he pointed out that Brown might be surrounded there, that he was going into a "perfect steel-trap."[2]

Brown replied that he would take hostages from the leaders of the Northern Virginia community and that, if worse came to worst, he would use those hostages to barter his way to freedom in the mountains. Douglass shook his head, claiming that "Virginia would blow him and his hostages sky-high, rather than that he should hold Harpers Ferry an hour."[3] Brown continued to defend the plan, saying that this was the time to strike against the slave system. Douglass shook his head, where-upon Brown put his arms around him, saying, "Come with me Douglass. I will defend you with my life. I want you for a special purpose. When I strike, the bees will begin to swarm, and I shall want you to help hive them."[4] Douglass shook his head again and freed himself from Brown's embrace. The meeting was over.

As he turned to go, Douglass asked his companion, a former slave named Shields Green, what he wanted to do. The answer he received has been quoted in many books since:

"I b'leve I'll go wid de ole man."[5]

Brown's 20 companions had grown by one.

Striking
the First Blow

The best account we have of the preparations for the raid comes from Osborne P. Anderson, one of the few raiders who survived the event. His *Voice from Harpers Ferry* was published in Boston in 1861.

MOTHER AND FATHER

Knowing it was essential to project an air of normal country life, Brown asked his daughter Ann and his daughter-in-law Martha to come to the Kennedy Farm. They arrived in the midsummer of 1859 and acted as scouts and lookouts, as well as cooks and washerwomen. The 21 conspirators and their leader spent most of their time in the attic of the Kennedy farmhouse, while Ann and Martha shooed away nosy neighbors. There was one in particular, a Mrs. Huffman, who was a perfect pest,

Osborne Perry Anderson, a free-born follower of Brown from Chester County, Pennsylvania, was the only surviving African-American member of the raid. Anderson went on to write about the event in his book *A Voice from Harper's Ferry*. Later he joined the Union Army and fought in the Civil War.

continually showing up unannounced, but the women managed to keep everything quiet. Anderson commented:

> Every morning, when the noble old man was at home, he called the family round, read from his Bible, and offered to God most fervent and touching supplications for all flesh; and especially pathetic were his petitions in behalf of the oppressed. I never heard John Brown pray, that he did not make strong appeals to God for the deliverance of the slave.[1]

The men went upstairs, to knit, sew, and discuss their plans, while the girls washed dishes and cleaned downstairs. The men began to call Watson Brown and his wife Father and Mother, and the presence of the young women made the long days in the attic more bearable. For their part, the women were most worried about Old Brown. Brown had become more haggard; he demonstrated fatigue, and, at times, a good deal of sadness.

This state of affairs continued until the last week of September, when Brown sent the women home. The house then became rather forlorn, with 22 rather desperate men waiting for the hour to strike. The Old Man, as they called him, said they had to wait until the crops had been harvested, for that was a time when slave discontent was at its highest. The Old Man did not tell them that he was despondent over the small number he had; he had hoped for two or three times as many volunteers.

There was plenty of discussion, and debate, among the volunteers. Most of them knew the desperate nature of their cause, and many were convinced that they would not return alive. On one occasion, Charles Tidd broke from the others after a long argument and left the house. He lived elsewhere for a week before returning to the fold.

Other concerns loomed over their heads. Brown was furious to learn that some of the men had sent letters home to their sweethearts, revealing parts of the plan. If everyone did this, the plan would be foiled.

By mid-October, Brown had given up hope for more volunteers. All his efforts had brought only 21 men to him. But there was no thought of turning back. This was the plan he had first announced to Frederick Douglass, 12 years earlier. Even though Douglass had not joined at the critical moment, Brown was ready to go ahead without him.

So, at last, the morning came when the Old Man declared that this was the day they would strike the first blow. It was October 16, a Sunday, and Brown typically commenced the day with a Bible reading. He also had some of his new recruits listen to the Chatham Constitution. Then everyone simply lay on their arms to pass the hours.

SETTING OUT

At eight o'clock that night, the Old Man said, "Men, get on your arms, we will proceed to the Ferry."[2]

They went two by two, with Brown in the lead. Everyone had specific orders about all sorts of possible situations that might arise. Should they encounter anyone on the road, they must detain them. Happily, this did not happen, and the little band of 22 came to the bridge over the Potomac River around 10 that night. Behind them, two men had been assigned the very important task of cutting telegraph wires; they did this work so well that there was no telegraphic signal from the area for the next 24 hours.

The Old Man and his men came across the Potomac Bridge and captured William Williams, the one guard at the bridge. Williams recognized John Cook and thought the matter a joke until he was bound and taken prisoner. Brown and his men knocked, rather loudly, at the federal armory gate. The guard there, Daniel Whelan, described what followed:

> I think there was about twenty-five men; they asked me to open the gate. I told them I could not open the gate by any means. "Open the gate," said they; I said, "I could not if I

was stuck," and one of them jumped up on the pier of the gate over my head, and another fellow ran and put his hand on me.[3]

Not waiting for a key, Brown's men used a crowbar and a large hammer to get through the iron gate.

At this point, Brown sent five men south, with specific orders to capture Colonel Lewis Washington and as many of his slaves as could be found. Brown wanted Colonel Washington because of his connection to George Washington. To make doubly certain that everyone would understand the importance, Brown gave a specific instruction concerning General Washington's sword:

In the case of Colonel Lewis Washington, who had arms in his hands, he must, before being secured as a prisoner, deliver them into the hands of Osborne P. Anderson. Anderson being a colored man, and colored men being only *things* in the South, it is proper that the South be taught a lesson upon this point.[4]

Before daybreak, Aaron Stevens, Osborne Anderson, and the others had returned. Colonel Washington was a prisoner. The opening stage of Brown's revolution had gone almost entirely according to plan.

THE FIRST MISSTEP

Around two in the morning, the regular Ohio-Baltimore train arrived from the west. This train always passed through Harpers Ferry, then across the railroad bridge to the Maryland side. Brown's men halted the conductor and his train, but, in the confusion, the first casualty occurred. It was a free black man, Shepherd Hayward, who was the regular night porter for the train. Hayward was fatally shot in the back. Everyone, from the participants in the raid to those who commented on it after-

Robert E. Lee was given command of soldiers and ordered to arrest those involved with the raid. By the time Lee arrived, 8 of Brown's 22-man army had been killed. Lee would later be promoted to general and command the Confederate armies during the Civil War.

ward, noted the terrible irony that the first person to be killed was an African American.

For the next few hours, the train was held up. Then, around four in the morning, Brown learned of the train's arrival. He told his men to allow it to pass through, but the conductor—fearing the bridge had been booby-trapped—decided to wait until daylight. Even though the conductor waited, letting the train leave proved to be a mistake. After the train continued its journey, the conductor halted it at a nearby town and sent a telegram to railroad officials. Both his telegram message, and the handwritten notes of some of the train passengers, suggested that 100 to 200 insurgents had control of Harpers Ferry and that hundreds of blacks had come to join them.

The news reached Washington, D.C., by 11 in the morning, and President James Buchanan had a quick meeting with John Floyd, the secretary of war. Both men were completely taken by surprise; neither had had the slightest inkling that something like this might take place. Floyd had received a warning from a

ROBERT E. LEE AND THE VIRGINIA MYSTIQUE

To this date, Robert E. Lee's life had been about as different from John Brown's as one could imagine. The only similarity is a connection to the Revolutionary War.

Brown's grandfather had served in the Continental Army, dying in 1776. Lee's father, Colonel Henry "Light Horse Harry" Lee, had served under George Washington with great distinction. But Henry Lee's promising beginnings had turned to dust. Falling into debt, he was imprisoned for two years later in life, and he died after a period of self-imposed exile in the Caribbean.

Young Robert Lee (born in 1807) was a paragon of virtue, from an early age. One suspects that his mother told him not to be like his father; if so, he strictly followed that command. Lee graduated second in his class at the United States Military Academy, or West Point, and accumulated no demerits in his four years there.

Quaker in Iowa a month before, but he had put the note aside, thinking it the work of a deranged mind.

Buchanan and Floyd both felt rather nervous about what could happen in the capital city, which had plenty of slaves. The immediate need, though, was to contain events at the Ferry. There happened to be no federal troops in the capital on October 17, so Buchanan and Floyd sent off an order for U.S. Marines from Annapolis. To command them, Floyd chose none other than Lieutenant Colonel Robert E. Lee.

Lacking time to change, Lee headed off on a train to Harpers Ferry, still wearing civilian clothes. His aide was Lieutenant J.E.B. Stuart, later a cavalry commander of great importance in the Confederate cause. On this particular morning, however,

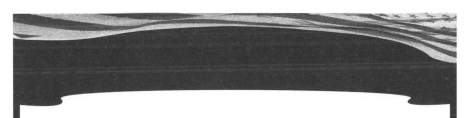

Returning home as a lieutenant of engineers, he married a member of the Washington family (making him a distant relative to Colonel Washington). Lee went on to serve with great distinction in the U.S.-Mexican War and to earn high praise from commanders and peers alike.

Lee was 52 when he was summoned to Harpers Ferry. He had not yet accumulated the final layer of grandeur that was to characterize his years as leader of the Army of Northern Virginia, but in his dispatches to the secretary of war one can feel the beginning of this legacy. Better than any other Confederate commander, Lee personified the virtues of being a Southern gentleman. He was calm and courteous, and had a quiet sense of humor. If John Brown personified the driven features of a Northern Yankee, then Lee exemplified the Southern qualities of charm and hospitality.

Lee and Stuart were both loyal members of the United States Army, dispatched to put down a rather strange, and alarming, rebellion at the Ferry.

THE SECOND MISSTEP

By eight in the morning, Brown and his men were nervous. They had succeeded in many of their objectives, yet there was no spontaneous arising by the slaves. About 40 slaves were with the rebels, but only a few of them could really claim to have joined on their own accord. Even the pikes, which Brown and his men thrust into their hands, seemed strange to them.

At first light, Brown sent a man to the nearby Wager Hotel asking for breakfast for his men and his hostages (he claimed that he needed none for himself). The hotel owner obliged, sending over heaps of food, but this was the last sign of good-will that Brown would receive.

By mid-morning, there were arguments between Brown and some of his men. Aaron Stevens, for one, was sure that the time was ripe to get out of Harpers Ferry. Though he did not quote Frederick Douglass's words, the idea of a "perfect steel-trap" was making itself known to Stevens and some of the others. Brown did not seem to know what to do. Even one of his most devoted admirers, Osborne Anderson, commented that "Captain Brown was all activity, though I could not help thinking that at times he appeared somewhat puzzled."[5] That puzzlement came from the lack of black slaves; Brown had sincerely believed that his raid would trigger a massive uprising.

Then the trap sprang shut.

JEFFERSON COUNTY

All during the early morning hours, riders had hastened through the countryside, bearing the news that Harpers Ferry was captured. Some of the riders took on, within their neighborhoods, qualities of Paul Revere. By mid-morning, militia companies were assembling throughout Jefferson County, and

Pictured is the engine house where Brown and his men were trapped. The engine house became known as John Brown's Fort. It is now part of Harpers Ferry National Historical Park.

just a few minutes before noon, Brown and his men heard the tramp of more than 100 footsteps coming across the Potomac Bridge. Hoping against hope that these were the feet of liberated slaves, Brown and a handful of men hastened to the head of the bridge, only to see that these were Virginia militia. A few well-timed rifle shots forced the militia to take cover, giving Brown some breathing room. But the escape—if it had ever been viable—was now closed.

Brown went among the prisoners he had collected overnight (there were about 40 in all). He chose them one by one and brought about 15 in all to the engine house, which stood right at the entrance to the federal arsenal. Colonel Lewis Washington was the most prominent of the hostages, but there were others who were known throughout the county; Brown believed their presence would give him safety, at least for the moment. But, as so many times on October 17, he judged wrongly. Anderson reported Brown's next move:

> Captain Brown next ordered me to take the pikes out of the wagon in which he rode to the Ferry, and to place them in the hands of the colored men who had come with us from the plantations, and others who had come forward without having had communication with any of our party. It was out of the circumstances connected with the fulfillment of this order, that the false charge against "Anderson" as leader, or "ringleader," of the negroes, began.[6]

There were, at most, 50 newly liberated blacks at the Ferry, and they were there from a variety of motives. Brown's men had compelled some to come, while others had come of their own accord. A few of them seemed keen for a fight, but the majority milled about with pikes in their hands and did not contribute to the defense.

By now, the raiders had lost several of their number. Dangerfield Newby had been shot in the throat and killed instantly. The angry militia used his body for target practice, shooting time and again and running bayonets through the corpse.

What went on in Brown's mind in these hours? He kept no journal of the events. The best guess is that he had stepped in over his head. While he was capable of masterminding an excellent first blow—the taking of Harpers Ferry—he was not enough of a captain, or general, to plan out the next move. All along, Brown had fervently believed that African Americans would rise as one when they had the opportunity. Now that optimism seemed misplaced, Brown was sitting in the "perfect steel-trap" of which Frederick Douglass had warned.

Reaping the Whirlwind

L ee reached Washington, D.C., by noon on October 17, and by two in the afternoon he and a group of 120 U.S. Marines were in railroad cars, grinding their way to Harpers Ferry. Meanwhile, the various Virginia and Maryland militia groups had boxed John Brown and his insurgents into a very restricted perimeter.

SWAPPING SHOTS

Beginning at noon, on October 17, the two sides swapped hundreds, if not thousands, of musket and rifle shots. The Virginia militia had Brown's company tied down at the arsenal, but in direct shootouts, the insurgents proved superior, time and time again. Perhaps it was the quality of the Sharps rifles that Brown used; then again, it may have been a higher level of training, but Brown's men gave more than they took on most occasions. The blood that they spilled only increased the rage of the crowd. A local physician, called to attend to the wounded, later described part of the action:

> I saw part of the fight at Hall's works. I went to put on some dry clothes at half past three o'clock, and that fight was then over. A yellow fellow was brought down on the bank of the river and citizens were tying their handkerchiefs together to hang him. . . . Kagi was killed, and a yellow fellow, Leary, was wounded and died that night; and the yellow fellow Copeland was taken unhurt.[1]

Yet another error John Brown made was to divide his already slender force. He and the main group held the engine house at the gateway to the arsenal, while John Kagi and three others held Hall's gun works, about 300 yards (274 meters) away. The Virginia militia overpowered Kagi's group, killing the leader, and soon Brown's insurgents were reduced by four of their number.

Back at the engine house, Brown felt troubled and confused. His plan was falling apart, and his only idea was to send out two men, under a flag of truce. Their proposal was that Brown and his men should be allowed to proceed, unharmed, to the Maryland side of the river, where they would release their hostages. But the citizen militia, which was becoming rowdier by the minute, would not have it. The flag of truce was fired upon, and Brown's men beat a hasty retreat.

The owner of the Wager Hotel had sent over many plates of breakfast to Brown and his men, but by noon the hotel had become the center of militia activity. Whether the owner provided free drinks (or whether they were paid for) is not important; what matters is that the militia became more and more drunk as the day progressed. The influence of alcohol undoubtedly contributed to the level of savagery. The true tipping point came when Fontaine Beckham, the mayor of Harpers Ferry and

Once Brown and the raiders were trapped in the engine house, they exchanged fire with the local militia. From this point on the raid worsened. Although Brown sent out his son Watson and his second in command, Aaron Stevens, with a white flag, the militiamen were enraged. Watson and Stevens were shot and wounded.

a man almost universally beloved, was shot by one of Brown's insurgents. Beckham had just told some townspeople to stay away from the scene, when he, overeager to have a look, was shot in the chest. He died instantly.

Beckham's death turned the militia into a mob. For the rest of the afternoon, the militiamen wandered the streets, occasionally firing random shots (it is something of a miracle that more civilians were not hurt). Three of Brown's men made a run for it. One got to the north side of the river and escaped. Another was caught, shot, and heaved over the railroad bridge, while a third, halfway across the Potomac River, was cornered by a militiaman. Don't shoot, he cried out. The militiaman gave a savage grin and blew the man's face away with one shot.

For the rest of the afternoon, the militia vented its anger on one or two helpless bodies, firing round after round into them. The mood was ugly—to say the least—and the few sober men in the area feared the whole thing would turn into a bloody massacre. If Brown had ever been in control of events, he had lost that control by now.

NORTH OF THE RIVER

Early in the morning of October 17, Brown had dispatched John Cook and two others north, to safeguard the Kennedy Farm and to raise the slaves of that region. They had Colonel Washington's four-horse wagon.

On their way north, Cook and the others came across Terrence Byrne, a neighbor who knew Cook well. He was astounded when first Cook, and then another man, pointed Sharps rifles at him, taking him prisoner. Before long, Cook had reached the one-room schoolhouse, where Lind Currie had 25 to 30 students. As Currie later recounted:

> He came in and demanded possession of the schoolhouse. He said he was going to occupy it as a sort of depot for their arms; that they intended depositing their arms and implements of war there; and they brought them in. At the same time he did not want me to dismiss the school. He thought I had better keep on the school and we should not be interrupted.[2]

This was, of course, absurd. The schoolchildren were quite alarmed, and Mr. Currie dismissed them for the day, telling them to take the straightest routes home. Currie himself walked a 10-year-old boy (who had no close neighbors) home, then returned to the schoolhouse to find Cook and the others in full possession. When they heard rifle fire coming from the Ferry, Currie asked Cook what it meant: "'Well,' said he, 'it simply means this: that those people down there are resisting our men, and we are shooting them down.'"[3]

From the volume of rifle fire, Cook and Currie might have thought there were hundreds of men in the area, and Currie asked how many were involved, Cook replied that there might be 5,000 or even 10,000 fighting each other. On later questioning, however, Cook admitted that John Brown's group was quite small. He went on to state: "We, as a little band, may perish in this attempt, but . . . there are thousands ready at all times to occupy our places, and to step into the breach."[4]

This was a common delusion on the part of Brown and the raiders. They could not bear to think that they had stepped into the breach alone, with no one following behind.

EVENING

Afternoon turned to the dusk of evening, but there was no letup in the violence. If anything, the militiamen, now numbering several hundred, turned even nastier. Most of them were thoroughly drunk; some continued to pepper the dead bodies of Dangerfield Newby and William Thompson with rifle fire.

By now, Brown's desperate plight had come to the attention of everyone except the Old Man himself. Brown still held out hope that relief would come, whether from the four men north of the river or from hundreds of liberated slaves from the south. Instead, the resolution came from the appearance of the U.S. Marines.

Robert E. Lee and 120 Marines arrived at Harpers Ferry at about eleven o'clock on the night of October 17. In his official report, Lee later claimed he would have made an immediate assault, had it not been for the hostages within the engine house. As it was, Lee and his men waited for morning, while Brown and four other men—Edwin Coppoc, Dauphin Thompson, Shields Green, and Oliver Brown—held out at the engine house. Oliver Brown was badly wounded, and all through the night he made noises, sometimes asking his father to kill him and put him out of misery. According to the testimony of several hostages, Brown continually replied with

On the morning of October 18, while the hostages were still in the engine house, Brown and his men fired upon J.E.B. Stuart and the Marines as they battered the door with a ladder. By this point, several of Brown's men had been killed, including his sons Oliver and Watson. It took only three minutes for the Marines to overtake the rebels and release the captives.

words of encouragement, followed by orders to die like a man. Sometime in the night, Oliver Brown made no more sounds, and his father commented that he must be dead.

Every half hour or so, Brown called out, "Men, are you awake?"[5] The reply was always in the affirmative, but the tiny band knew how overwhelmed it would be when morning came. Eventually the sky opened, and Brown saw the forces of his foe drawn up, within 100 feet (30 meters) or so of the engine house. Then came a lieutenant, by the name of J.E.B. Stuart.

LAST STAND

Stuart came to the door of the engine house, and met a shotgun held by the Old Man. Brown asked Stuart what he had come for, and Stuart presented Colonel Lee's demand for surrender, in writing. In the one-paragraph letter, Lee told the insurgents that they were completely surrounded, there was no way out. If they would yield the hostages and lay down their arms, at once, their lives would be spared.

Brown dismissed this overture, answering that his terms remained the same as the day before. He and his men must be allowed to leave Harpers Ferry, to get to the north side of the Potomac River, whereupon he would free the hostages. Nothing less would do.

Stuart stepped back a pace, and waved a handkerchief, his signal for the attack. Brown slammed the door shut, not a moment too soon.

A dozen U.S. Marines went at the main door to the engine house with hammers, but it held, even after a number of blows (Brown had craftily tied ropes to the door, so it would move, but not break, under such an attack). Seeing the futility, a dozen other Marines picked up a large ladder and attacked the main door. This time it broke, and seconds later the first Marines were within Brown's lair. One Marine was shot dead as he entered, and another was wounded, by the time Lieutenant Israel Green, a highly athletic man, got into the engine house and atop one of the engines. He was deciding whom to attack, when Colonel Lewis Washington, still a hostage, stood up to call out, "This is Osawatomie."[6]

Jumping from the engine top, Lieutenant Green was on Brown in a moment. He slashed at Brown with his saber, but the dress sword snapped after meeting Brown's belt buckle. Furious, Green went after Brown with the flat of his sword, and seconds later a U.S. Marine gave Brown two sharp wounds with his bayonet.

By now, the other rebels were all dead, and the hostages were liberated. Law and order had prevailed over insurgency and rebellion.

SLAVE REVOLTS

Southerners were not, could not be, indifferent to the possibility of slave rebellions. Not only did classical history provide a number of stories (such as the Spartacus Revolt against Ancient Rome), but the South had seen several uprisings since the beginning of American slavery.

In 1739, hundreds of blacks participated in the Stono Rebellion of South Carolina, named for a river in that area. The rebels had come close to success, but their very achievement meant that the retribution was terrible; at least 20 slaves were executed, in all sorts of ways.

In 1800, Gabriel Prosser of Virginia started a slave uprising in that state. He had coordinated his plans very well, and it took a large conglomeration of Virginia militia to subdue the revolt. Again, the retribution was savage. Finally, in the summer of 1831, Nat Turner of Virginia tried the same thing. Using a sophisticated set of codes and messages, he put together a slave rebellion that numbered in the hundreds. Not only was this insurrection put down with great force, but Virginia and other Southern states promptly put into law a new set of slave codes, which made it difficult for slaves to gather in groups of more than three and virtually impossible for them to obtain reading material. Guns, and other weapons, were, of course, strictly off-limits.

OUTSIDE THE ENGINE HOUSE

Minutes later, John Brown and Aaron Stevens were brought outside, to lie on the grass. Both men were severely wounded, and there was the possibility they might die before being interrogated. Colonel Robert E. Lee watched his prisoners carefully, more from a fear that the civilian militia would murder them than anything else.

Hours later, Governor Henry Wise of Virginia arrived. More than one person present, and more than one historian since, commented on how much Governor Wise resembled Brown. A few years younger than the "Old Man," Wise was also a lanky man, with long, sometimes wild, hair; like Brown, he seemed not to care about his appearance. Again, like Brown, Wise was known for his impulsive desire for action. On learning that the U.S. Marines had had the honor of capturing the insurgents, Wise swore he would have given up his right arm—clear to the shoulder, he said—for *Virginia* militia to have stormed the engine house.

Hours after the raid was contained, Colonel Robert E. Lee wrote a report to Secretary of War John Floyd, describing the conduct of the militia troops, and his own U.S. Marines:

> The promptness with which the volunteer troops repaired to the scene of disturbance, and the alacrity they displayed to suppress the gross outrage against law and order, I know will elicit your hearty approbation. Equal zeal was shown by the president and officers of the Baltimore and Ohio Railroad Company.[7]

prompting and that of my Maker, or that of the Devil—which-
ever you please to ascribe it to. I acknowledge no master in
human form,"[3] replied Brown.

By now, the interrogators should have realized that they
were up against a master of the art of argumentation. Brown
had spent many long winter evenings—in Kansas and at North
Elba—arguing for the freedom of the slaves, and, time and
again, he expressed it as a war against slavery. The insurgent

A HIGHER LAW

In the winter of 1850, Senator William H. Seward of New York had
this to say about the Constitution and the federal government when it
came to slavery:

> The Constitution regulates our stewardship; the Constitution devotes
> the domain to union, to justice, to defense, to welfare, and to lib-
> erty. But there is a higher law than the Constitution, which regulates
> our authority over the domain, and devotes it to the same noble
> purposes. The territory is a part, no inconsiderable part, of the com-
> mon heritage of mankind, bestowed upon them by the creator of the
> universe. We are his stewards, and must so discharge our trust as
> to secure in the highest attainable degree their happiness. . . . Shall
> we establish human bondage, or permit it by our sufferance to be
> established? Sir, our forefathers would not have hesitated an hour.*

Seward gave this speech at the height of the controversy concerning whether California might enter the Union. At the time, in
1850, nearly all senators and representatives used the Constitution of
1787 to justify their opinions, one way or the other. Seward was the
first, and perhaps the only congressman that year to speak to what

was justified in stealing the property of the slaveholder, and the slave was justified in rebellion (though not in violence against the master's person). A volunteer from a militia group asked the next question:

"How many men, in all, had you?"

"I came to Virginia with eighteen men only, besides myself."

"What in the world did you suppose you could do here in Virginia with that amount of men?"

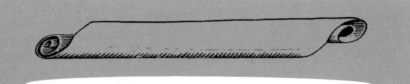

he called the "higher law," meaning a responsibility to humanity that was more important than the letter of the Constitution. He went on to quote Sir Francis Bacon, whom he described as one of the founders of modern philosophy:

> No man, says Bacon, can by care-taking, as the Scripture saith, add a cubit to his stature in this little model of a man's body; but in the great form of kingdoms and commonwealths, it is the power of princes and estates to add amplitude and greatness to their kingdoms. For, by introducing such ordinances, constitutions, and customs, as are wise, they may sow greatness to their posterity and successors. But these things are commonly not observed, but left to take their chances.**

In other words, Seward believed that the generation of 1850 must fulfill what the generation of 1787 failed to accomplish: the end of slavery.

The Works of William H. Seward, Vol. I. New York: Redfield, 1853, pp. 74–75.
**Ibid.

"Well, perhaps your ideas and mine on military subjects would differ materially."[4]

This became one of the thorniest problems for Brown's interrogators. While he was incriminated immediately, on the basis of his actions, his fearless attitude and presence made him seem morally superior to those who questioned him. Senator Mason went on to ask how Brown justified his actions.

"I think I did right, and that others will do right who interfere with you at any time and at all times. I hold that the Golden Rule, 'Do unto others as ye would that others should do unto you,' applies to all who would help others to gain their liberty," Brown replied.

Lieutenant J.E.B. Stuart broke in to say, "But you don't believe in the Bible."

"Certainly I do," was Brown's reply.[5]

The interrogation went on and on, with Brown winning more points by the minute. The more that his questioners pointed to his acts of violence, the more Brown asserted that he never meant to harm any innocent bystanders. The more that they cited Virginia and United States law, the more Brown referred to what many Northerners now called a "higher law" than the Constitution.

Brown's interrogators did not know how to change the subject or the point of their attack. The Old Man seemed to embarrass them, and to become their confidant, by turns. When he was asked about moral suasion, Brown scoffed, saying he had long since decided it was an inadequate way to end the sin of slavery. Late in the interrogation, an anonymous person asked:

"Brown, suppose you had every [slave] in the United States, what would you do with them?

"Set them free.

"Your intention was to carry them off and free them?

"Not at all.

"To set them free would sacrifice the life of every man in this community."[6]

Brown explained that he did not believe that was the case. Perhaps he had underestimated the willingness of the black slaves to fight, but he did not, he said, underestimate their willingness to pardon the slaveholders for the crimes they had committed.

Reporters from the *New York Times*, the New York *Tribune*, the Richmond *Enquirer*, and other papers hastened home to write up the conversation. There was no way to quarantine Brown's words, or the effects they had upon the nation.

THE REACTION

Whether they hailed from the North, South, or West, Americans were almost never indifferent to the Harpers Ferry raid. Southerners, almost universally, tended to see the raid as a flagrant violation of the many compromises that had been made over the decades between slave and free states. Here was a fanatical Northern man, who had doubtless obtained men, money, and guns from Northern merchants to invade the South. The Richmond *Enquirer* had this to say:

> The "irrepressible conflict" was initiated at Harpers Ferry, and though there for the time suppressed, yet no man is able to say when or where it will begin again or where it will end. The extent of this iniquitous plot cannot be estimated by the number of men detected and killed or captured at Harpers Ferry; the localities from whence these men came—from New England, from Iowa, from Ohio, from Kansas—show an extent of country embracing the whole Northern Section of the Union, as involved in the attempt at instigating servile insurrection in Virginia.[7]

Northerners were not as clear-cut in their thinking. Many admired Brown from a distance, but shrank from the kind of violence he had performed. Many remembered his terrible crime at Pottawatomie Creek and claimed he would have done the same at Harpers Ferry. Others believed that Brown was pointed in the right direction but that it would take someone more sane and rational to carry out his work. But there were others, especially in Concord and Boston, who admired Brown and the raid. The *New York Times* had this to say:

> These men will doubtless be hung for the crime they have committed. Conceding their guilt, it is not easy to complain of its penalty ... [but] we cannot think the ferocious tone generally held towards them by the Southern Press likely to be of service to the Southern cause. It only tends to make these men martyrs.[8]

Given the usual split between North and South, the opinions of Westerners became the crucial third. In the days that followed Brown's capture, Western newspapers did not make a definitive statement on the raid; the journalists and editors wanted the matter to unfold more.

BROWN'S TRIAL

John Brown went to court in Charles Town, Virginia (West Virginia, today) on October 25, 1859. Brown's appearance caused both trouble and surprise to those who wanted to see him executed. Old Brown—as he was becoming almost universally known—barely managed to walk into the courtroom. His vigorous physique, and what he called his abstemious (restraint from food and alcohol) habits over the years, had preserved his life, but the saber and bayonet wounds made him an object of sympathy to many in the crowd. Once inside, Brown was escorted to a mattress; he lay on the floor during most of the five days that followed.

There had been some discussion as to whether the Commonwealth of Virginia or the United States of America had jurisdiction in this matter, but President James Buchanan was glad to have Virginia do the work. The commonwealth's prosecutors opened their case by describing the manner of

Brown and the surviving rebels were arraigned on three state charges: treason against Virginia, inciting slaves to rebellion, and murder. Nearly 600 curious onlookers, including Northern newsmen, filled the court-room while the wounded Brown lay on a mattress. Brown's powerful testimony helped to convince thousands of Northerners that his actions were justified.

Brown's raid and the nefarious purposes he intended. His action could have resulted, they said, in the massacre of thousands of peace-loving Southern whites.

Brown's lawyer then countered with a plea for insanity. He brought forth evidence that Brown's mother had been insane, that one of his nieces was then confined to a sanitarium, and that Brown's first wife, Dianthe Lusk, had been insane. On the basis of all this mental illness in the family, he asked that the charges be dismissed. Brown, however, would have none of it:

> I look upon it as a miserable artifice and pretext of those
> who ought to take a different course in regard to me, if they

took any at all, and I view it with contempt more than otherwise. . . . I am perfectly unconscious of insanity, and I reject, so far as I am capable, any attempts to interfere in my behalf on that score.[9]

The judge agreed; the trial proceeded.

Until this point, John Brown and his fellow raiders had been on trial, but the two now became fused in the public mind. John Brown, Old Brown, Osawatomie Brown—whatever name he was called, Brown was on the minds of thousands, if not millions, of Americans. He did not disappoint.

Throughout the trial, Brown often appeared to be the person least concerned. He napped at times and only occasionally rose from the mattress to make a point or two. All he seemed concerned about was the matter of violence; he wanted the record to show he had not harmed any peaceful bystander. Other than that, Brown seemed content to go through what many people called a mockery of a trial.

The Commonwealth of Virginia did itself few favors during the trial. Had there even been an attempt at objectivity, had the judge and jurors shown more sympathy to an old man, they might have come off better in the public eye. Instead, Brown rapidly became the hero of a situation in which—to the eyes of most Southerners—he was a terrible villain. Many historians have tried to understand how Brown came off so well during the trial. Perhaps the best guess is that the Harpers Ferry raid really did frighten many white Southerners, frighten them so much that they rejoiced at the opportunity to gloat over Brown. That was a big mistake.

On November 1, 1859, the judge sent the jury to consider the evidence. They returned less than 45 minutes later, with a verdict of guilty. Brown was allowed some last words to the court:

Had I interfered . . . in behalf of the rich, the powerful, the intelligent, the so-called great, or in behalf of any of their

friends—either father, mother, brother, sister, wife, or children, or any of that class, —and suffered and sacrificed what
I have in this interference, it would have been all right; and
every man in this court would have deemed it an act worthy
of reward rather than punishment.[10]

But because he had acted on behalf of the powerless, Brown
was sentenced to death. He acknowledged that the court pro-
ceedings had been fair, and when he came to the question of
his own death, if it should speed the process by which millions
would be freed "so let it be done!"[11]

They won on all the technical points, while Brown won on
spirit and humanity.

DAYS IN JAIL

By the time he was sentenced, Brown had settled rather com-
fortably into the Charles Town jail. In the days and weeks
that followed, he became friends with his jailer, Captain John
Avis, who had led one of the militia groups that retook Harpers Ferry. Many people commented on the excellent goodwill
that prevailed between Brown and Avis; it was so strong that
Brown gave his word he would not attempt to escape, and Avis
accepted it. But there was, from the North, a stream of letters,
followed by a stream of visitors.

The poetess Lydia Maria Child was one of the first to write
to Brown. A friend and acquaintance of Ralph Waldo Emerson
and the Concord Transcendentalists, Child disapproved of
Brown's violent actions, but she loved the man and what he
stood for. In a long letter, she asked his permission to come and
serve as his nurse. Brown replied:

My dear Friend: ... Allow me to name another channel
through which you may reach me with your sympathies
much more effectually. I have at home a wife and three
young daughters—the youngest but little over five years old,

the oldest nearly sixteen. I have also two daughters-in-law, whose husbands have both fallen near me here.... Now, dear friend, would you not as soon contribute fifty cents now, and a like sum yearly, for the relief of those very poor and deeply afflicted persons?[12]

Letters like these served to further the growing admiration for Brown. But his detractors had their day as well.

Only two people experienced any bitter, or harsh, words from Brown. One was Captain Henry Pate, who came to visit Brown in jail. Brown derided Pate's courage, remembering their encounter in Kansas, and Pate did his best to spread bad words about Brown. The other person was Frederick Douglass, who, by now, had escaped first to Canada and then to England. Only on rare occasions did Brown mention Douglass's name, but when he did, it was always with anger and not a little bit of contempt. The person who counted the most, however, was Brown's wife.

MARY DAY BROWN

Less is known of Mrs. Brown than of her husband. She was quite young when they married, and she appears to have borne up well under the difficulties of their life together, including the bearing and raising of 13 children. They had been newly wed when Brown made his lifetime commitment to the eradication of slavery, and she may have guessed the tribulations that would come their way. Now, in 1859, she wished to see her husband once more.

John Brown tried to prevent it. He sent her letters, asking her to remain in North Elba, to keep the family together. She came anyway, however, and on the evening of December 1, 1859, husband and wife saw each other for the last time.

Mary came at four in the afternoon, and the couple had four hours together before a major general of the Virginia militia said their time was up. When she first arrived, Mary was

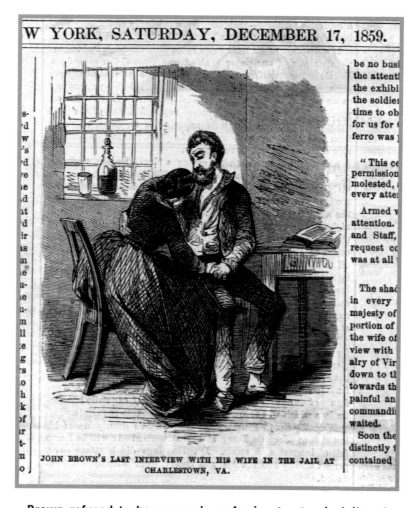

W YORK, SATURDAY, DECEMBER 17, 1859.

JOHN BROWN'S LAST INTERVIEW WITH HIS WIFE IN THE JAIL AT CHARLESTOWN, VA.

Brown refused to be rescued, preferring to stay in jail and become a martyr for the abolitionist cause. His letters from jail were picked up by the Northern press, gaining new supporters. *Frank's Illustrated Newspaper* depicts Brown's last visit with his wife, Mary. This was the only time Brown lost his composure.

much more emotional than her husband. He quieted her, and they talked for some time about practicalities; he wished to be buried in North Elba, for example. They also discussed the best way for their surviving children to be educated. Shortly before

Mary left, it was John Brown who broke down for one of the very few times in his life. For a few minutes he sobbed, then he kissed his wife and asked her to leave.

Brown wrote his will that night. All his property was left to his wife, with a few special keepsakes sent to his various children. His last letter to his family had been sent two days before:

> I am waiting the hour of my public murder with great composure of mind and cheerfulness, feeling the strong assurance that in no other possible way could I be used to so much advantage to the cause of God and of humanity.[13]

Brown's Last Days

J ohn Brown rose early on the second of December 1859. He knew this was his last day on earth.

Thousands of Northerners prepared to go to demonstrations and rallies on Brown's behalf. They, too, knew that his game was up.

Thousands of Southerners prepared to be part of the execution ceremony, and thousands of others prepared to celebrate. To them, Brown had become the embodiment of all that was wrong with the North.

DEPARTING

Brown left the jail around 10:30 in the morning. As he walked out, he handed a note to his jailer, Captain John Avis: "I, John Brown am now quite *certain* that the crimes of this *guilty land*: will never be purged *away* but with Blood. I had, *as I now think, vainly* flattered myself that without *very much* blood-shed; it might be done."[1]

Much controversy surrounds the next few moments. According to the early literature—written within a few years of the execution—Brown came out of the jail to see a sea of white faces, with just two exceptions, an African-American mother and her baby. According to legend, Brown paused, bent over, and gave the baby a sweet kiss. If this were true, it would go a long way toward amending Brown's public image, which could be frosty and hard, but those who study the event are almost certain that the kiss did not happen. The whites of Charles Town were greatly frightened of a possible rescue attempt on Brown's behalf; they had hundreds of soldiers in the area; and no civilian (let alone a black person) was allowed anywhere close to the prisoner.

Brown climbed onto the wagon. He sat on a large box in the middle, the box in which he would lie.

LAST JOURNEY

Brown had taken innumerable journeys in his long life. He had traveled from Connecticut to Ohio, from New York to Kansas, and from Kansas to Massachusetts, sometimes in the dead of winter. This last journey of his life took about 10 minutes. As they neared the execution spot, Brown remarked that the country was very beautiful; that he had never had the time to see it before.

Yes, was all the answer he received from Captain Avis, who was in a very glum mood. Like a handful of others who got close to Brown toward the end, Avis had fallen under the Old Man's spell.

The wagon stopped. Brown turned to Avis to say, "I have no words to thank you for all your kindness."[2] Avis replied with equal warmth.

Hundreds of Virginia soldiers were drawn up in squares. Hundreds of militia had been called in from other counties.

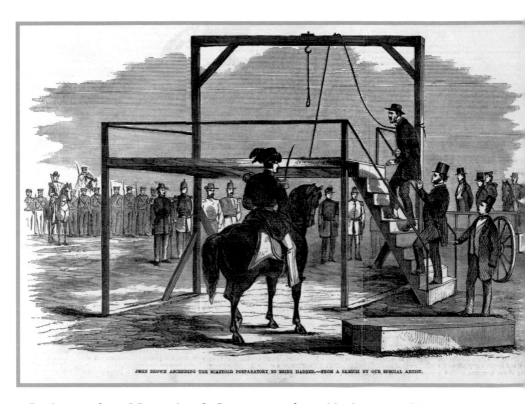

JOHN BROWN ASCENDING THE SCAFFOLD PREPARATORY TO BEING HANGED.—FROM A SKETCH BY OUR SPECIAL ARTIST.

On the morning of December 2, Brown—wearing a black coat and trousers, white socks, and red slippers—was escorted through a crowd of 2,000 soldiers that included Robert E. Lee and Stonewall Jackson. Authorities were concerned that Brown's sympathizers would attempt to rescue him.

Even a detachment of United States soldiers, commanded by Robert E. Lee, was present.

Brown walked toward the scaffold.

LAST MOMENTS

Brown made a special request that the execution be quick, but here he was foiled. Through some misstep by one of the executioners, he had to stand, blindfolded, for about 10 minutes before the trap door finally opened, and he swung like a common criminal. It took some minutes before he died.

The body was taken down, and, a short time later, it was given to Brown's widow.

Among the many observers were three men who would play a major role in the Confederate States of America. Robert E. Lee wrote a letter in which he decried Brown's last moments. Thomas "Stonewall" Jackson, who was but a militia captain at the time, wrote a letter to his wife, hoping that Brown had

SHAME OF THE SECRET SIX

With only one exception, the Secret Six turned out to be fair-weather friends. From the beginning, John Brown had won them over with his vigor and spirit, attributes they sometimes felt lacking in themselves. Nearly all of the Secret Six felt some connection to the Revolutionary War and the age of Washington, but only one, Samuel G. Howe, had ever acted in a heroic capacity, and that had been during the Greek Revolution, many years earlier.

After the raid, Howe and Franklin Sanborn promptly fled the country. They went to Montreal, Canada, where they kept up with American newspapers until they decided it was safe to come home again. Theodore Parker was in Italy, trying to regain his health (he died in 1860). No shame attaches to him, because Parker sent letters in support of Brown's actions. Gerrit Smith, the millionaire abolitionist who had given Brown land in upstate New York, entered a sanitarium, pretending to be insane. Frederick Douglass may have felt the most guilt of all.

To the end of his days, Douglass professed his admiration for Brown, once commenting that he had been willing to live for the slave but that Brown had been willing to die for him. In the weeks that followed the Harpers Ferry raid, Douglass fled, first to Canada and then for safety in England.

prepared his soul for the end. John Wilkes Booth was a recruit in the Richmond Greys militia unit. He later claimed that he looked upon the traitor with the utmost disgust and hatred.

THE CORPSE

Mary Brown received her husband's body within a few hours of his death. She began the trip home at once.

Mary Brown took her husband's corpse to upstate New York by train, but the last 100 miles (160 km) and more were over very rough roads, leading to North Elba. There, 10 days after Brown's execution, his body was laid to rest. The headstone of his Revolutionary War grandfather—which Brown had brought from Connecticut in 1857—was used for Brown and his son Frederick, who had been killed in Kansas. Six months later, on July 4, 1860, Osborne Anderson—one of the few to survive the raid—gave an impassioned talk to about 1,000 people at John Brown's grave.

THE FALLOUT

Brown was dead and gone, but the country was unable to let him rest in the grave; instead, every politician seemed determined to make the most—positive or negative—from his story.

Immediately after Brown's execution, every prominent Northern politician found it necessary to condemn the raid. William H. Seward of New York, Abraham Lincoln of Illinois, and numerous other Northern leaders roundly condemned Brown's methods, though they did not speak as strongly about his ideas. Southern politicians went much further, claiming that Brown was the advance man of a host of "Black Republicans," meaning that the Republican Party was behind Brown and would fight to continue his work.

Only the Concord Transcendentalists had much good to say about Brown. Henry David Thoreau gave an impassioned "Plea for Captain John Brown" to three different audiences in the autumn of 1859, pleading for the man's life and for a renewed belief in his cause. Ralph Waldo Emerson and other Concordites were more cautious, but it became apparent that they admired the man, even while deploring some of his methods. The South did not have an intellectual conclave like Concord, Massachusetts, but the bitter words from the Richmond *Enquirer* spoke volumes:

> The Harpers Ferry invasion has advanced the cause of Disunion, more than any other event that has happened since the formation of the Government; it has rallied to that standard men who formerly looked upon it with horror; it has revived, with ten fold strength the desire of a Southern Confederacy. The, heretofore, most determined friends of the Union may now be heard saying, "if under the form of a Confederacy, our peace is disturbed, our State invaded, its peaceful citizens cruelly murdered, and all the horrors of servile war forced upon us, by those who should be our warmest friends; if the form of a Confederacy is observed, but its spirit violated, and the people of the North sustain the outrage, then let disunion come."
>
> The people of New York have the opportunity, at the approaching election, not only of rebuking Mr. Seward, the great leader of the Ossawattomite Republicans, but of showing the people of the South, that the sympathy of the great State of New York is with Virginia and not with the traitor that must meet the just punishment of his treason.[3]

By the end of 1859, the United States had divided into three very different regions. There had always been the abolitionist North and the secessionist South, but now one added the militant West. Brown had spent part of his life in the Kansas Territory and the state of Iowa, and some of his strongest supporters had come from Ohio and Illinois. In the aftermath of his death, the Western states appeared to become closer to the Northern ones. No one was more aware of this than Abraham Lincoln.

Although many abolitionists viewed Brown as a sacrificial victim, Republican presidential candidate Abraham Lincoln and other members of his party tried to distance themselves from Brown, calling him a delusional fanatic. Historians claim that Brown's failed insurrection and the already tense relationship between North and South led to Lincoln's election and caused the Civil War to occur perhaps two decades earlier than it might have.

Lincoln was 50 when Brown was executed. His life had been a long uphill struggle toward the peace and prosperity he currently enjoyed. Had he been content, Lincoln could have remained a successful lawyer in Springfield, Illinois, staying out of the fray. But, by 1859, he had become a lukewarm abolitionist, meaning he believed that slavery must be contained where it was: that slavery must not be allowed to spread farther west.

In February 1860, Lincoln gave a speech at Cooper Union, New York City, one that many historians consider the most important of his career. Lincoln did not praise John Brown—indeed, he condemned his violence—but he struck enough of a note of friendship to stand for the new, emerging alliance between the abolitionist North and the Free State West. This was a line John Brown had tread through much of his life; though an ardent abolitionist, Brown had seen that abolitionists and Free State men must work together in the fight against slavery. Though Lincoln never admitted his intellectual debt to Brown, it was there for all to see.

Around the same time, the South became much more strongly secessionist, at least in tone. There was a difference between nullification (the idea that a state could nullify a federal law) and secession (the idea that a state could leave the Union entirely). Nullification had been much on the minds of Southerners during the 1830s, but in the late 1850s, they turned to secession. Their belief was that the Union had been formed as a gentleman's agreement between the 13 original states, and that, like a gentleman at a club, a state could choose to leave the Union at any time.

North, South, and West were all tense during the summer and fall of 1860. What would the elections show?

FOUR PARTIES

It was a four-way contest for the presidency. Abraham Lincoln won the Republican nomination in Chicago. Stephen A. Douglas, his opponent during the Lincoln-Douglas debates, won the Northern Democratic nomination. John Breckin-ridge of Tennessee won the Southern Democratic nomina-tion, and John Bell of Tennessee won the Constitutional Union Party nomination.

Not one of the four men was a confirmed abolitionist. Even though Lincoln was edging toward becoming one, he still spoke in qualified terms, suggesting that the North might have to stand back and wait as long as 100 years for slavery to disappear on its own. Stephen Douglas had always been indifferent on the matter of slavery. Breckinridge and Bell were neither confirmed secessionists nor Union men.

On November 6, Lincoln won the most of the popu-lar vote out of all the candidates. He won easily in the Electoral College, thanks to the split between the Northern and Southern Democrats. Stephen Douglas came in a distant second; Breckinridge after him; and Bell came in a very distant fourth. The voters had spoken.

SECESSION

Six weeks later, on December 20, 1860, a special South Caro-lina convention voted to secede from the Union. South Caro-lina removed the shackles that held it and took its place among the nations of the world.

One often forgets that it took some time for the Confederacy to assemble. For a few weeks, South Carolina stood all on its own, but by mid-February, it had been joined by six other states, and seven independent "nations" joined to form the Confederate States of America, with Jefferson Davis as its president. Meanwhile, Lincoln bided his time. He did not arrive in Washington, D.C., until just days before he delivered the Inaugural Address of March 4, 1861.

Lincoln went out of his way to reiterate that he did not wish to destroy slavery, and that he was not certain the federal gov-ernment had the power to do so. But on the matter of Union versus secession, he was crystal clear:

Physically speaking, we cannot separate. We cannot remove our respective sections from each other, nor build an impassable wall between them. A husband and wife may be divorced, and go out of the presence and beyond the reach of each other; but the different parts of our country cannot do this. They cannot but remain face to face; and intercourse, either amicable or hostile, must continue between them.[4]

Given that geographic fact, Lincoln asked, was it not better for North and South to reconcile, to patch up their differences? Toward the end of the address, he said, even more plainly, that North and South must remain friends. "Though passion may have strained, it must not break our bonds of affection."[5]

This was Lincoln at his best, in 1861. He was still a lukewarm abolitionist, but he, almost alone among the Northern leaders, had the political and emotional skills to bring about reconciliation. He did not, could not, invoke the recent memory of John Brown and the Harpers Ferry raid; to do so would ensure that virtually all the Southern states would flee the Union for the Confederacy.

The Power
of Song

Lincoln's best efforts failed. On April 12, 1861, Southern troops fired on Fort Sumter in the harbor of Charleston, South Carolina, beginning the momentous event we call the American Civil War.

VOLUNTEERS

The moment he learned of the Confederate attack on Fort Sumter, President Lincoln called for 75,000 volunteers to fight to hold the nation together. At this time, preserving the Union was his single greatest aim; only later in the war did Lincoln become a confirmed abolitionist.

Lincoln's call for volunteers was the last straw. Till then, several states of the slaveholding South had remained aloof from the Confederacy, but as soon as they learned of Lincoln's action, Virginia, Tennessee, North Carolina, and Arkansas left

John Brown's
ORIGINAL
Marching Song.

TUNE.—Brothers, will you meet me.

John Brown's body lies a-mouldering in the grave;
John Brown's body lies a-mouldering in the grave;
John Brown's body lies a-mouldering in the grave;
   His soul's marching on!

CHORUS.
Glory, halle—hallelujah!   Glory, halle—hallelujah!
Glory, halle—hallelujah!   his soul's marching on!

He's gone to be a soldier in the army of the Lord!
He's gone to be a soldier in the army of the Lord!
He's gone to be a soldier in the army of the Lord!
   His soul's marching on!

John Brown's knapsack is strapped upon his back!
John Brown's knapsack is strapped upon his back!
John Brown's knapsack is strapped upon his back!
   His soul's marching on!

His pet lambs will meet him on the way;
His pet lambs will meet him on the way;
His pet lambs will meet him on the way;
   They go marching on!

They will hang Jeff. Davis to a tree!
They will hang Jeff. Davis to a tree!
They will hang Jeff. Davis to a tree!
   As they march along!

Now, three rousing cheers for the Union;
Now, three rousing cheers for the Union;
Now, three rousing cheers for the Union;
   As we are marching on!

Johnson, Song Publisher, Stationer & Printer, No. 7
N. Tenth St., 3 doors above Market, Phila.

See Johnson's New Catalogue of Songs.

the Union, bringing the total of Confederate states to 11. As a loyal son of Virginia, Robert E. Lee resigned from his commission with the Union Army and soon rose to the rank of general in the Confederate armies.

Seventy-five thousand men came from the Northern states, soon to be joined by hundreds of thousands of others. Many were keen for the fight, but few realized how much blood and treasure would be spilled over the next four years. Like any new army, the regiments that came from the Northern states needed ways to bond, and the power of song soon emerged as one of the most important of all.

The details of how "John Brown's Song" came to be written are somewhat murky. Because the song and the tune were so flexible, soldiers changed the lyrics in all sorts of ways. To the best of our knowledge, the song was first sung by soldiers of the Massachusetts 12th Regiment. Once their fellows heard it, the song began to pass from mouth to mouth, and the first formal publication came in the New York *Tribune*, on July 28, 1861:

> *John Brown's body lies a moldering in the grave*
> *John Brown's body lies a moldering in the grave,*
> *John Brown's body lies a moldering in the grave,*
> *His soul's marching on!*
> *Glory Hally Hallelujah! Glory Hally Hallelujah! Glory Hally*
> *Hullelujah!*
> *His soul's marching on!*

(Opposite page) "John Brown's Body," also called "John Brown's Song," originally referred to a Sergeant John Brown of the 2nd Battalion of Boston's volunteer militia. Later, people mistakenly believed it was about abolitionist John Brown and added verses to reference him. It became a famous Union marching song during the Civil War.

The fourth verse made reference to Brown's lifelong love of animals:

His pet lambs will meet him on the way—
His pet lambs will meet him on the way—
His pet lambs will meet him on the way—
They go marching on!

The sixth tried to cap all that had gone before:

Now, three rousing cheers for the Union!
Now, three rousing cheers for the Union!
Now, three rousing cheers for the Union!
As we are marching on![1]

To say that this song had power is an enormous understatement. Perhaps it was the way the song fit in so well with marching bands; perhaps it was because the Union men simply loved it; but "John Brown's Song" became a nearly universal favorite.

The South had a powerful song of its own, "Dixie," or "Dixie Land," but it never attained the kind of power associated with "John Brown's Song." "Dixie" had a more joyful, almost civilian-like tone, while "John Brown's Song" echoed with the kind of man he had been, and the kind of men he had once told James Redpath he wanted: "Give me men of good principles, God-fearing men; men who respect themselves; and with a dozen of them, I will oppose any hundred such men as these Buford ruffians."[2]

The song changed that autumn. Julia Ward Howe, the wife of Samuel Gridley Howe, was with her husband and a handful of friends, outside Washington, D.C., in November. Their little party had to evacuate the area, because of a possible Confederate attack. On the way back to Washington, they sang "John Brown's Song" to each other, and one member of the party said to Mrs. Howe that he thought she should put it to her own set of lyrics. She replied that she had been thinking that very thought, and sometime that night, she awoke, unable to get back to sleep. In the early morning hours, she penned what became the "Battle Hymn of the Republic":

> *Mine eyes have seen the glory of the coming of the Lord*
> *He is trampling down the vintage where the grapes of wrath*
>   *are stored*

THE RAIDERS

What happened to the 21 men who went to Harpers Ferry with John Brown? Jeremiah Anderson was there at the last moment, defending the engine house. He was killed by a bayonet thrust from a U.S. Marine. Osborne Anderson was one of the few to survive. He made it over the Potomac River and into Maryland. Two years later, his *A Voice from Harpers Ferry* was published.

Oliver Brown died during the night of October 17–18. His brother, Watson Brown, survived the attack and was carried outside, where he died soon after. The others who died in the raid were John Kagi, Lewis Leary, Will Leeman, Dangerfield Newby, Stewart Taylor, Dauphin Thompson, and Will Thompson.

John Cook escaped from Harpers Ferry, only to be captured in Pennsylvania and returned to Virginia (he was hung in January 1860). Others who were executed for their role in the raid were John Copeland, Edwin Coppoc, Shields Green, Albert Hazlett, and Aaron Stevens.

Besides Osborne Anderson, four others escaped from Harpers Ferry and were never captured. They were: Barclay Coppoc, Francis Merriam, John Brown's son Owen, and Charles Tidd.

He hath loosed the fateful lightning of His terrible swift sword
His truth is marching on

I have seen Him in the watch-fires of a hundred circling camps
They have builded Him an altar in the evening dews and damps
I can read His righteous sentence by the dim and flaring lamps
His day is marching on[3]

The song was published in the *Atlantic Monthly* in February 1862, and Julia Ward Howe received $5 for her anonymous contribution.

Soldiers continued to sing "John Brown's Song" throughout the war, and they made many adaptations to it. But "Battle Hymn of the Republic" came to equal and then surpass it in popularity, so that by the end of the Civil War, the image of John Brown and his lambs had been replaced by the one of Christ and his terrible swift sword. Only a handful of songs throughout human history have been so effective at crystallizing a movement. "La Marseillaise," the song generated by the French Revolution, is as powerful as the "Battle Hymn of the Republic," and "Das Deutschlandlied" with its first line "Deustchland über alles (Germany above all)" had a great effect on the German soldiers of World War I and World War II. But in its coupling of a spiritual message with a political one, and in its presentation of God as the avenging angel, "Battle Hymn of the Republic" is nearly unique.

LEGACY OF JOHN BROWN

Brown was controversial in his own lifetime, and he remains so today. One of the most argued questions is whether Brown was a freedom fighter or a terrorist. Most historians take one of the two positions, while conceding that the other point of view has validity. Perhaps Brown deliberately fashioned his actions so as to continue the conversation. How else to reconcile a man who

THE FIFTEENTH AMENDMENT.
CELEBRATED MAY 19ͭ 1870

John Brown's goal to see slavery abolished finally was achieved with the passing of the Thirteenth Amendment. The Fourteenth and Fifteenth Amendments went even further and provided citizenship rights and voting rights to blacks. This poster depicts a parade surrounded by portraits of black life and rights granted by the Fifteenth Amendment. There is a picture of John Brown in the lower right corner.

could invade a town and take its leading people hostage, while claiming that he never meant to harm anyone?

Recent Brown biographers have emphasized the dual aspects of his nature. David S. Reynolds points to the admiration that some, perhaps only a few, Southerners had for Brown. His daring attempt at Harpers Ferry seemed to echo the daring of the Revolutionary War commanders. This appealed to the romantic spirit of the Old Dominion. Later in life, Viginia governor Henry Wise astounded one fellow Southerner by saying, "John Brown was a very great man, a very great man, sir!"[4]

Perhaps the best way to assess Brown's legacy is through a series of questions:

Would the Civil War have taken place if John Brown had not lived?

Almost certainly.

Would it have come as soon as it did, in the spring of 1861?

Perhaps not.

Would the causes of Union and emancipation have become so firmly entwined were it not for John Brown and the songs?

Perhaps not.

LEGACY OF HARPERS FERRY

When it took place, the raid on Harpers Ferry seemed like a madcap scheme, the product of a deranged mind. How did John Brown ever think, people asked, that he and 21 accomplices would bring down the slave power of the South?

Even a year later, when Lincoln was elected, many Northerners chose to keep a distance from Brown and his legacy, for they did not wish to be associated with a madman. But in the months that followed Lincoln's election and the weeks that followed his inauguration, Brown and the raid started to stand out as a lightning rod, as a symbol that pointed the way to Civil War and the liberation of the slaves. The Emancipation Proclamation, issued on September 22, 1862, truly fused the separate causes of the Civil War; from then on, Northern men fought for the Union and the liberation of the slaves.

Brown and his 21 accomplices started the train rolling, the one that rolled all the way to Appomattox Court House and the defeat of the slaveholding South.

CHRONOLOGY

1800 John Brown is born in Torrington, Connecticut, on May 9.

1820 Brown marries Dianthe Lusk. They will have seven children together.

The Missouri Compromise is passed, prohibiting slavery in the former Louisiana Territory north of Missouri's southwestern border.

1832 Dianthe Lusk Brown dies shortly after the death of their newborn son.

1833 Brown marries 16-year-old Mary Day of Meadville, Pennsylvania. They will have 13 children together.

1847 Brown meets abolitionist and escaped slave Frederick Douglass in Springfield, Massachusetts.

1850 Congress passes the Compromise of 1850, a series of statutes that attempts to balance the interests of slave states and free states. The fourth statute, the Fugitive Slave Act, declares that all runaway slaves must be brought back to their masters. This is a major setback to abolitionists.

1851 Brown organizes League of Gileadites, an organization founded to resist slave catchers.

1854 **May 24** Pro-slavery authorities attempt to make an example of fugitive slave Anthony Burns by arresting and jailing Burns in Boston, Massachusetts, before sending him back South. This causes many passive New Englanders to join the abolitionist cause.

May 30 Kansas-Nebraska Act allows settlers in the territories to determine if they would allow slavery in the newly created lands of Kansas and Nebraska.

1855 Brown's sons leave for Kansas to join the Free Staters. They write to Brown about the pro-slavery forces attacking anti-slavery supporters. Brown leaves for Kansas.

1856 **May 21** Border Ruffians burn down the Free State Hotel, destroy two newspaper offices, and ransack homes and stores in Lawrence, Kansas.

May 22 Senator Charles Sumner, leader of the anti-slavery forces in Massachusetts, is assaulted by South Carolina Congressman Preston Brooks in the Senate.

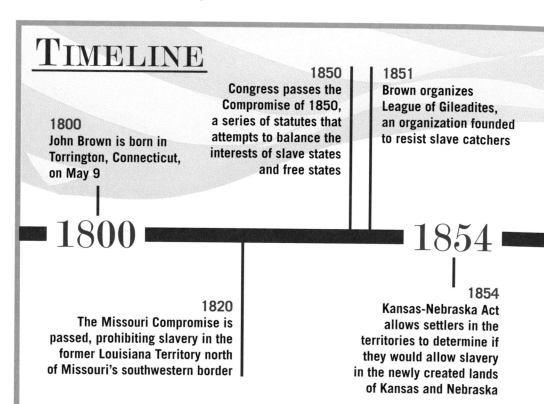

TIMELINE

1800
John Brown is born in Torrington, Connecticut, on May 9

1820
The Missouri Compromise is passed, prohibiting slavery in the former Louisiana Territory north of Missouri's southwestern border

1850
Congress passes the Compromise of 1850, a series of statutes that attempts to balance the interests of slave states and free states

1851
Brown organizes League of Gileadites, an organization founded to resist slave catchers

1800

1854

1854
Kansas-Nebraska Act allows settlers in the territories to determine if they would allow slavery in the newly created lands of Kansas and Nebraska

May 24–25 In the middle of the night to the early morning, John Brown and a group of men, including four of his sons, massacre five pro-slavery men at Pottawatomie Creek.

June 2 John Brown and 22 other pro-slavery soldiers defeat Colonel Henry Pate at the battle of Black Jack. This is Brown's first battle victory.

August 30 After thousands of pro-slavery Southerners march into Kansas and form armies, Brown and 38 of his followers engage 400 pro-slavery soldiers in the battle of Osawatomie. Hostilities continue for two months and Brown leaves Kansas. A fragile peace settles over the region.

1858
Brown organizes the Chatham Constitution, which would create a government for a new state with Brown as commander in chief

1859
Brown and his men attack Harpers Ferry. They surrender after the U.S. Marines surround the engine house and break down the door. Brown is hanged on December 2

1861
Civil War begins on April 12; "John Brown's Song" becomes a famous Union marching song during the Civil War

1856

1863

1856
John Brown and a group of men massacre five pro-slavery men at Pottawatomie Creek; Brown and 22 other pro-slavery soldiers defeat Colonel Henry Pate at the battle of Black Jack

1863
Lincoln passes the Emancipation Proclamation in two parts, declaring freedom to all slaves in those states that seceded from the Union

1857   Brown meets transcendentalist leaders Ralph Waldo Emerson and Henry David Thoreau.

March 6 Dred Scott Supreme Court decision declares that people of African descent are not protected by the Constitution because they are not American citizens.

1858   Brown organizes the Chatham Constitution, which would create a government for a new state with Brown as commander in chief.

1859   **July 3** Brown rents a farmhouse in Maryland in preparation for the raid of Harpers Ferry.

October 16 Brown and his guerrilla team begin their attack on the Harpers Ferry armory. They easily capture the armory and round up hostages, including Colonel Lewis Washington. The plan begins to go awry when a train baggage master, a free black man, becomes the first casualty.

October 17 Local militia seizes the bridge, blocking the escape route. Brown and his accomplices are trapped at the engine house.

October 18 U.S. Marines, led by Robert E. Lee, surround the engine house and break down the door. Brown surrenders and is struck several times in the head.

October 26-November 2 Brown goes on trial for treason in Charles Town and is sentenced to hang.

December 2 Brown's hanging is observed by 2,000, including Robert E. Lee, Stonewall Jackson, and John Wilkes Booth.

1860   **November 6** Republican Abraham Lincoln is elected president of the United States.

December 20 In response to Lincoln's election, South Carolina is the first state to secede from the Union. Ten other states follow.

1861   **April 12** Civil War begins between the North and the South. It lasts until 1865.

   July 28 "John Brown's Song" is published and becomes a famous Union marching song during the Civil War.

1862   Publication of "Battle Hymn of the Republic."

1863   Lincoln issues the Emancipation Proclamation in two parts, declaring freedom to all slaves in those states that seceded from the Union.

NOTES

CHAPTER 1

1. Testimony of Lewis Washington, "Harpers Ferry Invasion," *Senate Documents*, 36th Congress, 1st Session, p. 30.
2. Ibid., p. 32.
3. Ibid.
4. Ibid.
5. Ibid., p. 34.
6. Ibid.
7. Ibid.
8. Ibid.

CHAPTER 2

1. Daniel D. Hartzel and James B. Whisker, *The Southern Arsenal*, Bedford, Pa.: Old Bedford Village Press, 1996, p. 21.
2. *Seventh Census of the United States: 1850.* Washington: Robert Armstrong, Public Printer, 1853, p. 258.
3. Ibid.
4. Louis Ruchames, *A John Brown Reader*, New York: Abelard-Schuman, 1959, p. 36.
5. Ibid., p. 38.
6. Ibid.
7. Ibid.
8. Ibid.
9. Frederick Douglass, *Autobiographies*, New York: Library of America, 1994, p. 715.
10. Ibid., pp. 717–718.
11. Ibid., p. 719.

CHAPTER 3

1. Ruchames, *A John Brown Reader*, p. 76.
2. Ibid.

3. Ibid., p. 86.
4. William E. Connelley, *A Standard History of Kansas and Kansans*, Chicago: Lewis Publishing Company, 1918, p. 519.
5. *John Brown's Holy War*, PBS Video, 2000.
6. James Redpath, *The Public Life of Capt. John Brown*, Boston: Thayer and Eldridge, 1860, p. 113.
7. Ibid., p. 114.

CHAPTER 4

1. Redpath, *The Public Life of Capt. John Brown*, p. 309.
2. Ruchames, *A John Brown Reader*, p. 111.
3. Ibid.

CHAPTER 5

1. Douglass, *Autobiographies*, p. 758.
2. Ibid., p. 759.
3. Ibid.
4. Ibid., p. 760.
5. Ibid.

CHAPTER 6

1. Osborne P. Anderson, *A Voice from Harpers Ferry*, Boston, private printing, 1861, reprinted by Books for Libraries Press, 1972, p. 24.
2. Ibid., p. 31.
3. Testimony of Daniel Whelan, "Harpers Ferry Invasion," *Senate Documents*, 36th Congress, 1st Session, p. 43.
4. Anderson, *A Voice from Harpers Ferry*, pp. 30–31.

5. Ibid., p. 36.
6. Ibid., p. 37.

CHAPTER 7

1. Testimony of John D. Starry, Harpers Ferry Invasion," *Senate Documents*, 36th Congress, 1st Session, p. 27.
2. Testimony of Lind F. Currie, "Harpers Ferry Invasion," *Senate Documents*, 36th Congress, 1st Session, p. 55.
3. Ibid., p. 57.
4. Ibid., p. 59.
5. *John Brown's Raid*, Washington D.C.: National Parks Service, 1978, p. 43.
6. Ibid., p. 66.
7. Report of Robert E. Lee, "Harpers Ferry Invasion," *Senate Documents*, 36th Congress, 1st Session, p. 43.

CHAPTER 8

1. Ruchames, *A John Brown Reader*, p. 118.
2. Ibid.
3. Ibid., p. 119.
4. Ibid.
5. Ibid, pp. 119–120.
6. Ibid.
7. *Richmond Enquirer*, quoted in the *New York Times*, December 7, 1859.

8. "The Virginia Trials," *New York Times*, October 25, 1859.
9. Redpath, *The Public Life of Capt. John Brown*, p. 309.
10. Ruchames, *A John Brown Reader*, p. 126.
11. Ibid.
12. Ibid., p. 347.
13. Redpath, *The Public Life of Capt. John Brown*, p. 365.

CHAPTER 9

1. Ibid., p. 159.
2. Ibid., p. 399.
3. Ibid., p. 402.
4. Davis Newton Lott, *The Presidents Speak*, New York: Henry Holt and Company, 1994, p. 143.
5. Ibid., p. 145.

CHAPTER 10

1. *New York Tribune*, July 28, 1861.
2. Redpath, *The Public Life of Capt. John Brown*, p. 114.
3. Deborah Pickman Clifford, *Mine Eyes Have Seen the Glory: A Biography of Julia Ward Howe*, Boston: Little Brown and Company, 1978, p. 240.
4. Barton H. Wise, *The Life of Henry A. Wise of Virginia*, New York: Macmillan, 1889, p. 247.

BIBLIOGRAPHY

Anderson, Osborne P. *A Voice from Harpers Ferry*. Boston: Private printing, 1861, reprinted by Books for Libraries Press, 1972.

Ayers, Edward L. *In the Presence of Mine Enemies: The Civil War in the Heart of America, 1859–1863*. New York: W.W. Norton, 2003.

Carton, Evan. *Patriotic Treason: John Brown and the Soul of America*. New York: Free Press, 2006.

Clifford, Deborah Pickman. *Mine Eyes Have Seen the Glory: A Biography of Julia Ward Howe*. Boston: Little Brown and Company, 1978.

Connelley, William E. *A Standard History of Kansas and Kansans*. Chicago: Lewis Publishing Company, 1918

Douglass, Frederick, *Autobiographies*. New York: Library of America, 1994.

Eighteenth Annual Report Presented to the Massachusetts Anti-Slavery Society, reprint 1970. Negro Universities Press.

Gougeon, Len. *Virtue's Hero: Emerson, Antislavery, and Reform*. Athens, Ga.: University of Georgia Press, 1990.

"Harpers Ferry Invasion," *Senate Documents*, 36th Congress, 1st Session.

Hartzel, Daniel D. and James B. Whisker. *The Southern Arsenal*. Bedford, Pa.: Old Bedford Village Press, 1996.

Jefferson, Thomas. *Notes on the State of Virginia*. New York: The Norton Library, 1954.

John Brown's Holy War, PBS Video, 2000.

John Brown's Raid, Washington, D.C.: National Parks Service, 1978.

Lott, Davis Newton. *The Presidents Speak*. New York: Henry Holt and Company, 1994, p. 143.

Nelson, Truman. *The Old Man: John Brown at Harpers Ferry*. Chicago: Haymarket Books, 2009.

Our Documents: 100 Milestone Documents from the National Archives. New York: Oxford University Press, 2003.

Redpath, James. *The Public Life of Capt. John Brown*. Boston: Thayer and Eldridge, 1860.

Reynolds, David S. *John Brown, Abolitionist: The Man Who Killed Slavery, Sparked the Civil War, and Seeded Civil Rights*. New York: Alfred A. Knopf, 2005.

Ruchames, Louis. *A John Brown Reader*. New York: Abelard-Schuman, 1959.

Seventh Census of the United States: 1850. Washington: Robert Armstrong, Public Printer, 1853.

Simpson, Craig M. *A Good Southerner: The Life of Henry A. Wise of Virginia*. Chapel Hill: University of North Carolina Press, 1985.

Wise, Barton H. *The Life of Henry A. Wise of Virginia*. New York: Macmillan, 1889.

The Works of William H. Seward, Vol. I. New York: Redfield, 1853.

Further Reading

BOOKS

DuBois, W.E.B. *John Brown*. New York: Modern Library Classics, 2001.

Earle, Jonathan. *John Brown's Raid on Harpers Ferry: A Brief History with Documents*. Bedford/St. Martin's, 2008.

Koestler-Grack, Rachel A. *Abraham Lincoln*. New York: Chelsea House, 2009.

McNeese, Tim. *Robert E. Lee*. New York: Chelsea House, 2009.

Renehan, Edward J. Jr. *The Secret Six: The True Tale of the Men Who Conspired with John Brown*. New York: Crown, 1995.

Sterngass, Jon. *Frederick Douglass*. New York: Chelsea House, 2009.

———. *John Brown*. New York: Chelsea House, 2009.

Woog, Adam. *The Emancipation Proclamation*. New York: Chelsea House, 2009.

FILM

John Brown's Holy War, PBS Video, WGBH Educational Foundation, 2000.

WEB SITES

The American Experience: John Brown's Holy War

http://www.pbs.org/wgbh/amex/brown/

The Web site for the 2000 PBS film, featuring information on the program as well as the people and events related to John Brown.

Harpers Ferry National Historical Park

http://www.nps.gov/HAFE/index.htm

A comprehensive description of the place, John Brown's Raid, and its importance in American history.

John Brown State Historic Site, Oswatomie, Kansas

http://www.kshs.org/places/johnbrown/index.htm

The home of Brown's half-sister and brother-in-law; also the base from which he operated during the Bleeding Kansas period.

The Kennedy Farmhouse

http://www.johnbrown.org/

A complete overview about "the staging area" for John Brown's raid on Harpers Ferry. The farmhouse has been restored with federal, state, and philanthropic funds and is a National Historic Landmark.

Photo Credits

INDEX

ABOUT THE AUTHOR

SAMUEL WILLARD CROMPTON teaches history at Westfield State College, in the Berkshires of his native western Massachusetts. He is the author or editor of many Chelsea House books, including *Ulysses S. Grant* and *Alexander Graham Bell*. He grew up playing Avalon Hill war games like "Gettysburg," but he had little idea that the much-smaller action at Harpers Ferry had so much to do with bringing on the great war of 1861–1865.